The Playing Card Oracles

The Playing Card Oracles

A SOURCE BOOK FOR DIVINATION

Ana Cortez

Illustrations and Essays by C. J. Freeman

TWO SISTERS PRESS

Kind acknowledgment is made for permission to reprint
quotations on the following pages:
> page 21 courtesy of Shambhala Publications, Inc.
> page 24 courtesy of Parabola
> pages 105–6 courtesy of Quest Books
> pages 133–4 courtesy of CRCS Publications.

Typesetting and production management by Argent Associates, Boulder
Printing by Data Reproductions Corporation, Auburn Hills

Cover art by C. J. Freeman
Cover design by Alan Bernhard, Argent Associates
Author photo by Walkabout Studio

Two Sisters Press
P.O. Box 5613
Santa Fe, NM 87502

www.anacortez.com

Library of Congress Control Number: 2002092274
ISBN: 978-0-9719861-0-7

Printed in the United States of America

This book is dedicated to my father, C. J. Freeman.

> Dad, I imagine us in a storybook
> somewhere, our little ship set sail
> against a sky of dreams.
> And where will our little ship go?
> Only the Two Sisters know!
> It's true, "Treasure maps are always torn
> in two," because it is in the bringing
> together that lies the treasure.

This book is also dedicated to Freeman and Nanette,
the lights of my life. I love you guys.

Acknowledgements

ALL MY THANKS TO ...

Lainy, wherever you are. I'll never forget you.

Laddy, your enthusiasm and support came just when I needed it. You kept the flame alive.

Jessica, what would we have done without you? Your editorial expertise and unfailing belief in this project have been our guiding star.

Mary M., for your hard work, your humor, and your friendship.

Marcus, for being my best student and helping me to refine many important ideas.

Ron Becker, for untold hours of personal sacrifice. My dad loves you.

Linda and Patty and all the good people at Lithographic Arts, for going above and beyond.

Lisa McD., for being the most flexible boss in the world.

Alan at Argent Associates, for making the seemingly impossible possible.

My family, your love and support mean all the world to me.

My grandmother Jayne, one of my personal heroes. This book would not be here without you.

I would also like to thank Joan Raye, Maryanne and Julie, Freddie and Rob, Karen O., M. E. Ford, Scott Lyon, Steve Lyons, Roxanne Koehler, and all the many unnamed who have contributed along the way.

By their numbers, suits, and pictures,
The Cards communicate
And begin to tell their story
Each time we shuffle Fate.

— C J F

$\mathscr{C}$ontents

BOOK TWO
Essays, Notes, and Commentary

Author's Note

IVINATION IS A WORD that refers to any number of methods designed to make known the will of the Divine. But this is not a divinity to be sought somewhere outside ourselves. It is divinity within. This is what makes it so wonderfully accessible. In divination we open ourselves to the voice of truth, present inside each of us, but muffled by the clang and clatter of our own reactions to life, our fears, and our conditioning.

Just as a person would not play a game of cards blindfolded, one would hardly choose to play the game of life without knowing their hand, so to speak, and yet people do this, metaphorically holding onto cards that should be discarded, passing when they should play, etc. My grandmother, an avid Bridge player and venerable old soul, once said that the real challenge in cards is to have a poor hand and play it well. As with life, the cards do not represent a sealed fate, but help us to make decisions with open eyes.

Introduction

ARD READING WITH PLAYING CARDS may seem like a strange proposition. After all, aren't playing cards for games? Think about the striking fact that there are 52 cards in a deck as well as 52 weeks in a year. Could this be merely a coincidence? Consider that the 52 cards are divided into 4 suits, just as the year is divided into 4 seasons, and that each season consists of 13 weeks, exactly as each suit consists of 13 cards.

Here's a simple exercise. Count up all the numbers in a suit, with Aces as one, 2s as two, etc., Jacks as eleven, Queens as twelve, and Kings as thirteen. What do you get? The answer is 91, the total days in a season. Add all the numbers in the deck and you get 364, a curious number that is just one and one-quarter days shy of a solar year. But what if the deck was never intended to represent a *solar* year?

A look through history reveals that the playing deck is actually a perfect replica of a Fixed Lunar Calendar. This very simple model of timekeeping predates solar calendar systems like the Gregorian one we now use. Based on the observation of natural rhythms, the Fixed Lunar Calendar consists of thirteen cycles of twenty-eight days each, or exactly 364 days.

When you think about it, a calendar provides a layout in which to chart events that have not yet occurred. It is a map of the future. Of all the features of the playing deck, these perfect calendar correlations are perhaps the hardest to pass off as mere circumstance. Far from a haphazard creation, the construction of the deck alludes to a clearly thought-out intention, to a purpose far greater than ordinary gaming.

THE PICTURE BOOK OF ANA CORTEZ

THE CARD ILLUSTRATIONS that accompany this text are from *The Picture Book of Ana Cortez*. Be very clear that this is not a Tarot deck nor is it derived from Tarot in any way. It is a separate oracle entity all its own and speaks in its own distinct voice.

The deck is illustrated by my father, C.J. Freeman. His love for the playing cards and his wonderful intuition as an artist have produced innumerable revelations and endowed the so-called ordinary playing deck with extraordinary beauty. In my father's own words, "The drawings take their own courses. They have their own intelligence."

Over the past twenty-five years I have watched my father draw and re-draw playing cards, hundreds of them. His dedication is an inspiration. From chalks to oils to inks, the stream of images continues, ever-morphing, ever-evolving. *The Picture Book of Ana Cortez* is his third complete volume of work.

THE MAKING OF THIS BOOK

THE BOOK YOU HOLD IN YOUR HANDS is the result of a remarkable journey that began more than twenty years ago, a journey not of miles but personal discovery. There is magic in the seemingly ordinary playing deck we all grew up with, a whole enchanted world, just waiting to be discovered.

My first exposure to playing cards as something beyond an ordinary gaming deck happened at a fairly young age. I was perhaps thirteen or fourteen years old, on a visit to my father (my parents were divorced) when I ventured into his basement to find larger-than-life oil paintings of the cards. The paintings were my dad's first effort at illustrating the playing deck, his own self-assigned "art project." But this was like no art *I* had ever seen and certainly unlike any cards. The startling and vivid images on the canvases would have been a shock even for Alice as she wandered through Wonderland.

The strangeness of the pictures combined with the atmosphere in this particular basement produced a very surreal and memorable experience for me. The basement itself was little more than a hole, probably better described as a cave. The dirt floor and crumbling rock walls were cast in shadows, lit only by the single light bulb my father had hung to paint by. He showed me how he had written the names of my sister and myself into the lines of wrinkled fabric on two of the figures.

My fascination had been captured, but years passed and thoughts of playing cards drifted far from my mind. It wasn't until after graduation from high school when I went to live with my dad for the summer that the deck was reintroduced as something extraordinary. Excerpts from this period appear in later chapters of this book, describing experiences with a card reader named Lainy. Lainy was my father's girlfriend at the time, a woman with a dark, exotic look and the spirit of a gypsy to match. Dad had taught her some basic card reading techniques based on his own studies with the playing deck. Lainy took his ideas and put them into practice. For her readings she used a one-of-a-kind playing deck made from photographs of the images created in the basement years before.

Lainy and I spent most of our days together that summer, talking endlessly about life and cards. Through her eyes, I saw the playing deck as if for the first time. She introduced me to the incredible symbolism it contained and how the meanings could be applied to our daily lives. I began to understand that the cards held secret knowledge and took detailed notes. That summer was a turning point for me. My perceptions had changed, but I was young, and the bigger world was calling my name. Once again, cards drifted from my life.

Finally, more than ten years later, my fascination for the playing deck surfaced again, but with a greater seriousness than before. I had just been through a devastating life change that left me questioning almost everything I had experienced up to that time. I needed to find myself again. The cards would become my vehicle.

Fortunately, much of the material on my father's original system had been preserved by a woman who called herself Laddy LaDoux. Laddy, like Lainy, had learned card reading from my father and had been using his method for years. She was generous enough to share with me all she knew about the cards, and I was an eager student. As time went on, however, I became increasingly aware that the information I had collected was only one piece of a greater puzzle. All my notes somehow stopped short. The deck itself hinted at more.

This is when the fun began. I felt as though I were a detective on a classified mission. Books on calendar systems, the four elements, and alchemy began collecting around my house. I dusted off my old astrology and numerology texts and started to look into geomancy, a magical practice from the time of the Renaissance that has historical connections to playing cards.

An ongoing collaboration with my father during this period allowed an even greater depth of study. Two people focused on the same thing generate an energy difficult to create alone. Our conversations about cards spilled into the hours on many occasions. Discoveries were often surprising and appeared in unexpected ways: in dreams, for example, or through words spoken in a seemingly unrelated conversation. Gradually, a wondrous system of card reading emerged, beautiful and multi-faceted, like a shimmering jewel. This is what you will find in the pages that follow.

My hope for this book is that someday it will be acknowledged by people outside the card-reading and so-called "new-age" populations. Truly we are *all* in a new age. The world vibration is changing. At this fascinating and critical point in our human history, now is the time for information such as is contained in this book to become part of the general consciousness. The playing deck has slipped through our lives for many hundreds of years under a veil of ordinariness, its magic disguised by its simplicity and the fact that it can be used for games. May this book facilitate the lifting of the veil. It is time for Sleeping Beauty to awake.

ℋOW TO ᵁSE THIS ℬOOK

𝒯HE METHOD OF CARD READING disclosed in *The Playing Card Oracles* is the result of many years of study and discovery. It is not meant to be mastered in a short period of time. Take it in pieces, and practice, practice, practice. The text has been designed to take you step-by-step. Part One will introduce you to the basic language of the cards. Color, number, and suit meanings along with detailed descriptions for each of the 52 cards will provide the tools for your card reading toolbelt. Parts Two, Three, and Four will show you what to do with your tools. Card layouts and how to interpret them, reading techniques, and tips on tapping into your own intuitive power are covered at length and interwoven with sample readings throughout. BOOK Two provides an interesting perspective of playing card history.

One more note: if you acquired this book without its companion deck, *The Picture Book of Ana Cortez*, there is no need to worry. Find a deck of playing cards that you like and follow along. The regular deck is the root and source of this system of card reading and is no less an instrument for divination than the illustrated deck featured in *The Playing Card Oracles*.

Book One

PART ONE

Card Symbolism

PART ONE will open your eyes to the playing deck as never

before. Secrets will be revealed. Cards will come to life

before you as you enter their world of colors, suits, and

numbers. This part is your ABCs and 1-2-3s. Study it well.

Parts Two, Three, and Four will show you how to apply

what you have learned.

Calendar Correspondences

*A*LTHOUGH A NUMBER OF AUTHORS have mentioned the calendar correspondences in the playing cards, this book is, to my knowledge, the first published material on how to make practical use of it. The card spreads covered later in the text will show you how.

CALENDAR CORRESPONDENCES
WITHIN THE PLAYING DECK

52 cards	→	52 weeks in a year
4 suits	→	4 seasons in a year
13 cards in each suit	→	13 weeks in each season, 13 lunar cycles in a year
Total of numbers in each suit (counting Aces as 1, Jacks as 11, Queens as 12, and Kings as 13) = 91	→	91 days in each season
Total of numbers in the Deck = 364	→	364 days in the Fixed Lunar Year

---

As you take the deck into your hands, you are taking hold of a time machine. With each turn of the cards, weeks and months pass, seasons change, and a unique opportunity to glance into future or past unfolds before you.

The Magic of Three

HREE IS A PROMINENT NUMBER in many traditions of magic and prophecy and the 52-card deck is no exception. Three are the sisters who personify the three aspects of Fate, weaving their web of past, present, and future throughout the lore of many European traditions. Three are the phases of the moon: waxing, full, and waning, emblematic of the three stages of life as recognized in the Goddess practices. Three are the legs of the sacred chair upon which the Pythia of Delphi would sit as she uttered her prophecies of the future, and three are the components that make up the 52-card playing deck—*colors*, *suits*, and *numbers*. For this reason, we will refer to these three aspects of the deck again and again as we make our way through the text. In time, these pillars of understanding will take shape in your mind, erecting a temple of wisdom from which to draw insight for yourself and others.

COLORS

IF THE PLAYING CARDS ARE SO SPECIAL AND EXTRAORDINARY, then why aren't they full of color? Why the same old black, red, and white, century after century? In answering this question, we stumble on some of the more subtle mysteries contained within the cards. The limited palette of color used in the playing deck is one of simplicity, yet deep symbolic implication. In it we find yet another example of the number three and the power it has within the pack.

To the alchemists, the trinity of black, red, and white was the magical color combination that corresponded to the three essential phases of spiritual evolution. Black pertained to fermentation and repentance, white to transcendence and pardon, and red to suffering and love. Examples of this color trio appear repeatedly in the literature and art of religion and myth.

One more critical observation exists in terms of color. Because each card is either black or red (on a white background), we can view the deck as a binary creature. Binary means it is made up of two equal and contrasting or distinct parts, like yin and yang, yes and no, male and female. This additional correspondence opens up huge possibilities for interpretation and has far-reaching implications. Again, we see that less is more when it comes to color. To fully make use of the colors built into the deck, this book includes ideas on color interpretation (see *Looking for Black and Red*, p. 134) as well as geomancy, a sister system of divination that is based on just this kind of two-part observation.

NUMBERS

All things have a number,
and it is this fact
which enables them
to be known.

—PHILOLAUS, ca. 450 B.C.E.

NUMBERS ARE A FASCINATING AND COMPLEX FACET of the playing deck. By familiarizing yourself with the unique role that the numbers play within a reading, you will be getting to know them in a new way. They begin to take on life and meaning beyond their ordinary, one-dimensional counting or quantitative function. They begin to reveal their spirit.

Within the playing deck, there are two general categories of cards by number. Single-digit cards (Ace through Nine) are called pips, and double-digit cards are called courts.[1] "Pip" is the old card term for a suit sign (a Diamond, Club, Heart, or Spade) and a catchall word for cards that feature suit signs rather than court figures.

In numerology (the art and science of numbers), the single digits are sometimes referred to as the "original nine," as they truly are the only numbers that are original, all others being simply new combinations of them. Accordingly, it is the pip cards whose meanings embrace the spectrum of human experience. The courts, on the other hand, are a new breed of cards quite different from their predecessors. They are personalities, representing complex characteristics just as the numbers assigned to them are complex. They symbolize actual people within a reading.

The court figures can be conceptualized as the actors and actresses who play out the events and circumstances that are the pips. The pips are the lessons we must learn, the trials that shape our individual karma. Together, these two groupings work to represent all the diverse phenomena of human life.

The following gives an overview of the numbers 1 through 9 as they operate within readings. Seen collectively, they symbolize a grand unfolding. Notice how the characteristics of each number are born from the one before it and in turn give rise to the next. Each is separate only as stones of the same pathway are separate. Through the numbers, life can be understood as a thing in movement, a work in progress.

Insight into the nature of the court cards can be gained by studying the two numbers that appear on each, although I believe numerological interpretation to be of limited value here. As stated before, courts belong to a different group or order of cards separate from the pips. Their personalities are broad, archetypal, and potentially mystical.

---

[1] Among the court personalities featured in this card reading system you will find the "Lady Cards," long ago discarded from the court and labeled as simply a "ten." This upset the balance of male and female within the court and put a two-digit number in the faceless grouping of single digit cards. *The Picture Book of Ana Cortez* is, among other things, an attempt to rectify that situation. Further discussion on this topic can be found on p. 78 and in *Book Two*, pgs. 218-219.

Characteristics are entwined by gender, age, suit, and relationship to other members of the court. Each is a potential vehicle for *every* pip experience.

ONE (Ace): Self

Positive expression: powers and potentials contained within the individual

Negative expression: avoidance of manifestation, fear of losing self

TWO: Self and Other

Positive expression: partnership, cooperation

Negative expression: division, self against other

THREE: Manifestation

Positive expression: decision and movement

Negative expression: vacillation and worry

FOUR: Foundation

Positive expression: organization and completion

Negative expression: disorganization or rigidity

FIVE: Crossroads

Positive expression: opportunity and diversification

Negative expression: restlessness and confusion

SIX: Harmony
Positive expression: creation of harmony, experience of peace
Negative expression: complacency, fear of challenge or
disruption

SEVEN: Challenge
Positive expression: growth, development of inner strength
Negative expression: obstacles, destructiveness

EIGHT: Fortification
Positive expression: achievement, support
Negative expression: materiality, failure

NINE: Final Challenge
Positive expression: selflessness, humanitarianism
Negative expression: extremes and selfishness

SUITS

The Four symbolizes the parts,
qualities, and aspects of the One.

—CARL JUNG,
Psychology and Religion

THE SEASONS CYCLE ROUND AND ROUND, ever flowing, one to the next, ever renewing the life they contain. As part of nature, we too must dance to the shifting tune of the seasons' song. We wear the faces of youth, adolescence, mid-life, and old age. We embody the forces of mind, body, emotion, and spirit. It is this cycling, this exchange of form, that the suits of Diamonds, Clubs, Hearts, and Spades symbolize.

Each has its own personality, so to speak, its own inherent characteristics that aid in interpreting a spread of cards. The contrasts between the suits are vital, allowing each to supplement the others. They energize one another while tempering each other's extremes. Together they bring balance and wholeness to a spread.

The suit signs were fashioned as key symbols for core energies that manifest through the individual numbers, Ace through King. Inscribed upon unbound card "pages," their stories unfold. Suits mix and mingle, harmonize and clash, and finally reflect our experiences—inner and outer, past, present, and future. I can picture some kind of Creator seated on a grand throne, joyously shuffling and throwing spreads from a royal deck, creating the seemingly endless array of phenomena we call life. And now, allow me to introduce ... the suits.

DIAMONDS

MAGICAL NAME:	Ignita
ELEMENT:	Fire
DIRECTION:	South
SEASON:	Autumn
PHASE OF LIFE:	Mid-life
PRINCIPAL BODY PART:	Head
COMPATIBLE SUIT:	Clubs
KEY CONCEPTS:	Prosperity, Creativity, Self-confidence, Transformation, Spiritual growth

The sparkling Diamond, formed within dark Earth by intense pressure and heat, is a radiant symbol of transformation, representing well the spirit of the cards within this suit. Money is a major correspondence for Diamond cards and an essential tool of transformation on this Earth. Through its use, goods and labors are exchanged. One thing becomes another. For example, the work you put in at the office becomes your mortgage payment and your groceries. Diamonds represent prosperity or potential for prosperity.

Through our own spirituality, transformation can also be expressed, though an *inner* transformation as compared to the *outer* transformation symbolized by money. Spiritual potential, illumination, and consciousness are all concepts that fall within the realm of Diamonds, although not very commonly. Mankind has become so outwardly directed, using the power of Diamonds to generate money and earthly power rather than spiritual depth.

The personality of this suit is creative and inspirational. There is a need to reflect the inner experience in the outer world. Think again of the Diamond, and how light shining through it is refracted and beautified to reveal the colors of the rainbow. This is like life filtering through people who manifest this suit.

Fire is the Element of the Diamonds. Sitting next to a cozy hearth or even a burning candle, I notice my gaze is drawn again and again to the flame. Now imagine this same energy as it lives inside a person. People with strong Diamond characteristics are magnetic, compelling, and dynamic. Just as firelight banishes darkness, when we incorporate this suit into our lives, we take hold of an inner torch, lending courage and an ability to meet with confidence the circumstances that come our way. A lack of Diamonds can indicate a certain fearfulness or inability to trust. Life can be like walking into a dark room and not being able to find the light switch.

People "in Diamonds" tend to be rather "me" oriented. They do not like to be weighed down with heavy concerns for others. Watery feelings (Heart suit) threaten to dowse their Fire. Too many material or practical concerns (Spade suit) smother their creative impulses. The lighter, airy qualities expressed by the Club suit, however, complement the suit of Fire well. Clubs feed Diamond ambitions with new ideas and allow the freedom they need.

An overabundance of Diamonds in a spread is rarely seen as a problem by the person who has it. This is because Fire, in itself, is not sensitive. Commonly, only in hindsight is the imbalance recognized. The person can get literally "burned out" after being hopelessly driven to the point of exhaustion. Usually others in their path have been "burned" as well. Symptoms of this imbalance often manifest as self-centeredness, greediness, and/or an excessive concern for making things happen.

As with all the suits, balance must be sought. Each suit is kept in check by the presence of the other three. Diamond energy lights our life. Too little is a day without sunshine. Too much is a Fire that knows not its own bounds.

Every Fire possess a hunger

   Like none you've ever seen

   Set a feast before this creature

   And he'll lick each platter clean

   Never matters what you offer

   He's always wanting more

   See him eating up your ceiling

   And gobbling up your floor?

   Takes a day before he's finished

   And stops to catch his breath

   Done digested eighty acres

   But starved himself to death

                                        —CJF

CLUBS

MAGICAL NAME:	Ethra
ELEMENT:	Air
DIRECTION:	East
SEASON:	Summer
PHASE OF LIFE:	Adolescence
PRINCIPAL BODY PART:	Throat
COMPATIBLE SUIT:	Diamonds
KEY CONCEPTS:	Ideas, Thinking, Dreams, Communication, Detachment

The suit of Clubs represents many of the more subtle and elusive ener-gies of the pack. Corresponding to mental processes and the Element of Air, it symbolizes things unseen. People attuned to this suit work well within the realm of ideas and imagination. They are the inventors, the entrepreneurs, the dreamers. They conceive those things that are yet to be in our physical world.

Picturing now the Element associated with Clubs, further insight can be gathered into the nature of this suit. Air is our human ocean, our environment. By breathing we become intimately connnected to all other breathing creatures. Applying this then to a spread of cards, we can say that Clubs provide a sense of connection, of relationship. They bring understanding to the dynamics of a reading. Air is a soft, receptive Element. It harmonizes energies that might otherwise be antagonistic.

In keeping with this concept of subtle receptivity, it is important to recognize Air as a carrier. Air delivers sound to our ears and smells to our olfactory senses. Clubs are messengers and suggest an affinity for communication. They represent information, reading, writing, and verbal abilities. People with a strong show of this suit are typically fond of talking and social situations where they can relate to others on a mental level.

While these cards indicate connection, ironically they also reveal a sense of detachment gained from an ability to look at things from a logical perspective. As if strapped onto the back of a bird in flight, those with well-developed Club energy are able to view the bigger picture, separating themselves from intense personal involvement. Those of a less airy orientation are likely to perceive this kind of person as simply cold or uncaring.

Of the other three suits, Diamonds provide the best match for Clubs, sharing their love for the lighter side of life. As the Element of Fire, Diamonds mix naturally with the suit of Air, stimulating and putting into action Club ideas and dreams. When found together in a layout, these two suits symbolize an ease and flow not demonstrated between Clubs and either the Heart or Spade suits.

Spreads imbalanced by too many Club cards have substantially weakened energy. Strength is found in their alliance with other suits. Standing alone, Clubs represent ideas not carried through to manifestation. Like a mournful, restless wind, this suit of Air can become as a sad and discarnate spirit, a breath without a body. Conversely, when Club cards are missing from a reading, there is a need for mental stimulation and reflection on one's experiences and life in general.

You are not enclosed within your bodies,

nor confined to houses or fields.

That which is you dwells above the

mountain and roves with the wind.

It is not a thing that crawls into the sun

for warmth or digs holes into darkness

for safety.

But a thing free, a spirit that envelops the
　　Earth and moves in the ether ...
This would I have you remember in
　　remembering me.
That which seems most feeble and
　　bewildered in you is the strongest and
　　most determined.
Is it not your breath that has erected
　　and hardened the structure of your bones?
And is it not a dream which none of you
　　remember having dreamt, that builded
　　your city and fashioned all there is in it?
Could you but see the tides of breath
　　you would cease to see all else,
And if you could hear the whispering of
　　the dream you would hear no other sound.

　　　　　　　　—KAHLIL GIBRAN, *The Prophet*

HEARTS

MAGICAL NAME:	Agana
ELEMENT:	Water
DIRECTION:	West
SEASON:	Spring
PHASE OF LIFE:	Childhood
PRINCIPAL BODY PART:	Torso
COMPATIBLE SUIT:	Spades
KEY CONCEPTS:	Emotions (love, passion, hate, fear, etc.), Sympathy, Healing, the Subconscious

The Heart is one of those universal symbols that needs no words to explain. But more than simply "love," the suit of Hearts encompasses the full array of feeling and emotional possibilities. It represents our blood, our passion, and our pain. It is the reason we love and the reason we war, our reason to live and the causes for which we die. Its impulses bypass the mind, confounding attempts at logic and reasoning, originating in a place deep within our being.

This is the suit that corresponds to the Element of Water. Understanding this association is key to understanding the nature of these cards and how they behave within a spread. Water is nurturing, fluid. Washing ourselves with it, we are not only cleansed but renewed and refreshed. Heart cards in general symbolize these same qualities. Their presence within a reading points to healing and an ability to nurture and care for others, as well as oneself.

It is the graveyards near bodies of Water that have the most hauntings, giving a further clue into the nature of this Element. Water picks up and holds vibration. As such, Heart cards represent sympathetic energy. People manifesting Hearts are attuned to the undercurrents of reality, the feelings behind words spoken and unspoken. This is the suit representing those things that lie beneath the surface of conscious awareness.

Without a shape of its own, Water seeks solid forms to hold it and give it function. Be it the rocky bottom of a river bed, a cup from which to drink, or the veins and tissues of one's own body, this Element is gravitational and must conform to the confines of its vessel. As the suit that corresponds to Earth, Spades is the natural partner for Hearts in this way, giving this suit of the emotions both stability and purpose. Hearts, in turn, nurture and give life to Spade characteristics.

Diamonds, as Fire, present an exciting combination for Hearts, although a very unstable one. Fire touching Water will sizzle and steam, but eventually these two Elements eliminate each other. Club cards as they appear with Hearts in a reading symbolize a very sensitive dynamic as both these suits deal with finer, softer energies. This is also a more difficult association than the Hearts/Spades combination.

When Hearts is the dominating suit in a spread, the person you are reading is looking at life through the lens of their feelings. They possesses natural healing ability, although it can be latent or unexpressed. There is a natural attunement to subtle energies. Complications arise because with so much Water it is easy to get "washed away," to be so sensitive to feelings and moods that one becomes vulnerable to fears and insecurities of all kinds. As previously mentioned, the stability offered by the Spade suit is vital to Hearts and can help offset the difficulties that come about when this suit of the emotions is heavily represented.

Conversely, a lack of Heart cards corresponds to a lack of attention to feelings. Especially in our hustle-bustle, technologically oriented society, human sensitivity and emotion are often perceived as more of a hindrance than an asset. Because Hearts are related to healing, their absence often alludes to a *need* for healing. This becomes especially apparent when Spades are present in the spread. Spades without their companion suit of Hearts is Earth without Water. Think about what this means to the physical being. A healthy emotional state is vital to the health of the body. The section called *Generating Suit Energies* (p. 130) gives ideas on how to re-establish connection with the energy that the Heart suit represents. As always, a good balance of suit energies is the best medicine.

Of all the Elements, the sage should take Water as his preceptor. Water is yielding but all-conquering. Water extinguishes Fire, or, finding itself likely to be defeated, escapes as steam and reforms. Water washes away soft Earth or, when confronted by rocks, seeks a way around. It saturates the atmosphere so that Wind dies. Water gives way to obstacles with deceptive humility, for no power can prevent it following its destined course to the sea. Water conquers by yielding; it never attacks but always wins the last battle.

—from *The Wheel of Life*,
by JOHN BLOFELD, ©1972
Reprinted by arrangement with
Shambhala Publications, Inc., Boston

SPADES

MAGICAL NAME:	Terra
ELEMENT:	Earth
DIRECTION:	North
SEASON:	Winter
PHASE OF LIFE:	Old Age / Death
PRINCIPAL BODY PART:	Feet
COMPATIBLE SUIT:	Hearts
KEY CONCEPTS:	Labor, Career, Housing, the Physical Body, Discipline, Responsibility

A Spade is a dark thing, even more so, if possible, than its black counterpart, the Club. Clubs, being associated with the Element of Air, at least have a lightness, a levity about them. Spades, on the other hand, are associated with Earth, making their blackness heavy and dense.

The Spade is a tool, a weapon. For the gardener it is everything—the sharp blade that breaks the solid Earth to till and expose what nature has been brewing in darkness. For the warrior it is the all important spear point, an especially significant weapon back in the days when playing cards were conceived. Like the gardening spade, the spear point was made for thrusting, but for thrusting into flesh—another Earth, of sorts.

So, what do a gardener and a warrior have in common besides this all-consuming urge to thrust? They both *labor*. Spades is the suit of work, toil, and physicality. Where you find Spades in a spread is where you find that the person works hardest. It is the point where routine and even drudgery enter.

Compared to the Elements of the other three suits, Earth is relatively stable and permanent. It slows down the more volatile and excitable Fire, Air, and Water. As such, people with strong Spade tendencies demonstrate a dependability, predictability, and conservativeness not possessed by any other suit.

Intermingling most naturally and completely with Spades is the suit of Hearts. Spade characteristics provide security and stability for Hearts, which correspond to Water. Hearts supply the feeling qualities needed to soften Spade characteristics, just as Water softens and nurtures an otherwise dry and inhospitable Earth. I have always found it interesting that the Spade is an upside-down Heart with the addition of a little stem.

Diamonds and Clubs, of course, also have their own relationships with the suit of Spades, though neither demonstrates the same natural mix or balance as the Spade/Heart combination. Diamond cards present an energizing match for Spades within a reading (Fire and Earth), indicating a real "go-getter" dynamic; however, it is a very coarse pairing as both these suits run short on sensitivity. Motives can turn to greed and hunger for power if not kept in check. Clubs and Spades create an obviously very black combination that manifests as a dry, serious outlook lacking excitement or spontaneity.

Earth as an Element is unique in that it is form-bound. Its shape is deteriorated by time and must die to be reborn. In human beings, for example, we witness the degeneration of the physical body with age, as the emotional maturity and spiritual consciousness often improve. Accordingly, the vitality in Spades is found in youth while the rewards of the other suits typically emerge with age. Because court cards depict personalities as they progress through the different phases of life, you will find this aspect of the suits reflected there.

Looking at a cluster of Spade cards laid out on the table, I feel I am looking at a black, pointed army with spearheads poised, ready for battle. A lot of this suit within a reading signals conflict, clash, hard spots. Spades, as Earth, are dense and unyielding. A spread imbalanced by many Spade cards typically indicates situations of feeling trapped, boxed in. People with this feature tend to be stubborn, skeptical, and argumentative. On the other hand, people who have a weak show of Spades can be unreliable, flighty, and lacking in discipline.

Cards within this suit certainly represent more than their fair share of difficulty and challenge within the playing deck. Symbolizing physical realities, Spades address tough issues that must be dealt with in real terms.

The negative aspect of the stability of the Earth

is its inertia, the downward attraction of

gravity. A solid structure on Earth, even a

living body, requires upward energy to move.

It does not flow like Water or Air. When we

stood on two legs rather than four, it was in

defiance of Earth's gravity. The free legs

became arms that could aspire upward,

even to be raised in worship, attracted by

a higher force.

—Reprinted from *Parabola:*
The Magazine of Myth and Tradition,
Vol. XX, No.1 (Spring 1995)

The Oracles

The word oracle is derived from the Latin orare, *which means to speak.*

THE MEANINGS OUTLINED HERE will serve as your foundation. They are the alphabet of the craft. Just as musicians know musical notes and writers know words, card readers must know their cards. Memorize the meanings. Make them part of how you think.

Although they are meant to guide you, the correspondences brought to light in this section are not meant to be limiting in any way. Feel free to "color outside the lines" if your intuition directs. The cards are a tool only. What we are trying to get at is inside ourselves. Let the images on the cards provide the spark that lights this greater knowing.

As you read through the pages that follow, take time to notice that each card symbolizes several possible interpretations, occasionally even contradictory ones. This is because we are looking at the cards as they *stand alone*. Individual readings can and will differ greatly, and card meanings must be flexible. When placed within the context of an actual layout, surrounding cards provide a context, a lens from which to view its individual members. Time, practice, and interpretive techniques covered in other parts of this text will guide you in choosing which meanings to apply.

ACES

WHAT IS AN ACE? Is it simply the lowest numbered card in the deck or is it the most mighty? In games, we know that Aces can sometimes be considered low and sometimes high. The fact that they have been given the name of "Ace" instead of the rather plain-sounding title of "One" also gives testimony to the special qualities of these cards. Numerologically speaking, One is a special number. Not only is it the very first number (making it a bit brave!) but it also acts as the common denominator for every other number. Quite a job. As such, Aces symbolize incredible potentials; however, these forces are largely latent. You can think of them like seeds. They require certain conditions in order to come to fruition. Several Aces in a spread suggests that the person is containing all their talents and energies, resisting manifestation.

I remember giving a reading to a woman who had three out of four Aces showing. As it turned out, she was in her sixth year of college, working on her second degree, and planning on more school. Her energies were "incubating" and showed as multiple Aces. As they appear in a spread, these cards also reveal a keen awareness of the self and the powers contained within the individual.

Aces are like storehouses or energy sources for the particular suit they represent. Nearby cards within a spread can plug into and draw from an Ace, but only if the individual exercises that choice. For example, a Queen of Hearts next to an Ace of Hearts would be an incredible combination whereby the Queen personality could tap into the reservoir of Heart energy contained within the Ace, magnifying her own Heart vibration. The closer in proximity a given card is to an Ace, the more it can access this power. Same or compatible suits are naturally more able to blend in this way.

Aces represent the character of their respective suits in the most pure and complete way. They symbolize primal, fundamental force. Accordingly, you will find the magical names of the suits pictured on the Aces in *The Picture Book of Ana Cortez*.

*

A◆

Ignita

When looking at this card, notice how the large red Diamond in the center looks more like a gem than a traditional suit sign. If you examine it closely, you will see a figure silhouetted within its core. The story that follows illuminates the symbolism of this Ace. In it, the stone of "Philosophicus" is depicted as holding the secrets of the Element Fire. Like the volcano that fashioned the stone, the Ace of Diamonds contains an incredible and dynamic potential. As with all Aces, its power can be tapped into for use in our lives if that choice is exercised. The gifts awaiting here include the creative ability to will our dreams into reality as well as attract money and resources.

In the story, King Diamantis serves as a wonderful example of what *not* to do with the powers of this Ace. Remember, Fire is an Element that consumes. It is difficult to satisfy. Handled carelessly, the inner Fire can grow to become greed, egotism, and insensitivity. That is why the precious powers encapsulated within the stone are shown carefully guarded by a fearsome dragon, the archetypal protector of treasure. Draw from this Ace, illuminate and energize your world. Beware the hunger of its Fire.

- ◆ potentials for financial gain or creative endeavors
- ◆ a strong sense of self and a person's own individuality, the ego
- ◆ the will to do, to achieve
- ◆ spiritual values and transformation
- ◆ an engagement ring, a diamond

THE DIAMOND ACE: *A Story*

The stone Philosophicus was fashioned in the rumbling bowels of Mount Ank Dar when the ancient volcano was active on Yootmando, a small island off Tuskany. The stone was worshipped by islanders as a divine gift, for it seemed to burn by some unknown chemistry without combustion or heat to produce a glowing radiance called cold fire by the Yootmans. A strange lizard-like shape could be seen silhouetted in this amber transparency, as if some long extinct creature had been imprisoned within the stone. This creature or shadow resembling a creature was known as Philosophicus, the fire lizard.

Centuries passed before Diamantis, Sovereign Lord of old Tuskany, acquired Philosophicus from a Hundoogee chief descended from the legendary Yootmans. Diamantis prized this one stone above all his treasure and came to believe certain stories told about its powers. It was said the stone imprisoned a fire lizard that would bless whomever released it with immortality and great wealth.

Now Diamantis was old and coveted money. The more he thought about it, the more he believed in those wondrous stories told him by the Hundoogee. Finally, he could resist no longer and, taking his dagger hilt, Diamantis crushed the stone, releasing its prisoner.

Within seconds an incredible transformation occurred. Diamantis' skin turned luminous white, like hot metal. His eyes began to glow. The King's attendants were horrified and ran screaming through the palace and into the courtyard, crying leprosy.

One look at Diamantis was enough to chill the blood, and his court quickly abandoned him, leaving the palace uninhabited. Everything Diamantis touched turned radiant, then crystallized into a glowing mass. Finally, confused and terrified, the King appeared at a tower casement then plunged like a fiery comet from heaven to the earth below where his body literally shattered into a thousand pieces.

Upon examination, it was determined that Diamantis had indeed, by releasing the fire lizard, been blessed with immortality and great wealth, just as the Hundoogee had promised. His shattered body, every bone and pore, had been fired into Diamonds, the most brilliant, beautiful stones ever seen in all the realm.

Those in the Diamond Kingdom descend from Diamantis, which means Diamond in the old language, and, like their great forefather, they covet money and often amass much treasure. This is a kingdom ruled by the Element of Fire, which in ancient times was associated with transformation. The fire lizard, Philosophicus, can be a deadly, unstable force that rampantly destroys everything it touches. However, as the ancients also deduced, this is a divine agent that can benefit those who have wisdom and are prepared for its effects.

—CJF

A♣

This Ace is pictured as the Club itself wearing the cloak of a simple yet awesome moth of the imagination. The name on the card reads Ethra, the magical name for Air, but why the symbolism of a moth? A moth is a being who lives between imagination and reality, a creature nearly as light as the Air in which it lives, silent in flight and wearing almost non-colors. He represents another world, invisibly existing alongside our visible world of stone and mortar. Remember that the visible had its conception in the invisible, where dreams, ideas, and creative impulses have their being.

Our dreams burn bright like candles
  In a window seldom seen
  It's covered thick with ivy
  And latched until we dream.

The Ace of Clubs is pictured
  As a moth with dazzled eyes
  Who seeks the flame within us
  And burns brightly 'til he dies.
  —CJF

Ethra is an energy, an intelligence present within the Air we breathe. It is everywhere, connecting us all, penetrating all.

Born on the wings of breath, thoughts and ideas

- ♣ potential for communication, speaking, writing

- ♣ dreams or wishes

- ♣ the power of the mind, the power of believing

- ♣ that which is unseen, unmanifest

- ♣ premonition, prophecy

THE PICTURE BOOK OF MADAME ZO
extraordinary playing cards
© 2000 CJF

become words and sound. This Ace cries out for us to connect, speak, and believe. We need to pay attention to the voice that lives inside each of us. Take a moment to notice your breath, your sacred, quiet breath, and imagine all that you are connected to right now.

THE CLUB ACE: *A Story*

Morphoos, the fabled city of Clubs, was a wondrous hilltop metropolis that flickered like a star in an otherwise desolate sky near Lok Nork. Visitors dazzled by the city's radiance had to cover their eyes and often knelt before the inhabitants, mistaking them for angels. Truly a replica on earth of what heaven must resemble in all its glory, Morphoos was the ancient seat of Kings descended from Bell Zab.

According to legend, when Bell Zab fulfilled his promise to "marry not among the daughters of men," and had spent his life as a solitary shepherd, he was given dream children in old age. These children were born of his own body, after which a covenant was established between Bell Zab, a poor shepherd, and the god of his vision, a creature called Somlepid, or the Dream Moth. This covenant enabled Bell Zab and his direct descendants to materialize objects found in their dreams and build the wondrous city they inhabited. For generations, Bell Zab's descendants married among themselves and not among the children of men until the time of Mo Mut, Bell Zab's great grandson.

Captivated by earthly beauty, Mo Mut married a slave woman from Lok Nork who bore him children, whereupon the covenant established by Bell Zab was forever broken. The city of Morphoos totally vanished, leaving its inhabitants as if awakened from a pleasant dream, now faced with harsh reality.

The Club suit descends from Mo Mut and inherits his propensity for dreaming. However, Clubs are children born of the daughters of men and as such, they lack the power to transform dream images into material things. Like Mo Mut, Clubs are attracted to physical, earthly forms and often forfeit their true inheritance. The Kings of Morphoos could dream and by dreaming alone create a wondrous city, but Clubs must learn to act on their dreams and create with their own hands the bricks such cities require.

—CJF

A ♥

Agana

The large raptor pictured on this card is a striking symbol of obvious significance. It is said that the heart is a lonely hunter and, like this bird of prey, the heart must often seek out those things that fulfill its basic needs. It is a creature of desire, thirsting for and devouring affection, nesting where it finds love.

Another correspondence for this Ace is Water, Agana, in the sense of *inner* Water, our feeling life. Now take a moment and imagine the power and magnitude of all your emotions contained within the one Heart pictured on this card. The energy represented here is as a well of feeling so deep it is doubtful one could ever reach the bottom. Herein lie all the potential of love and devotion, passion, and compassion, as well as obsession, fear, and compulsion. Remember, this suit encompasses the realm of the subconscious, as hinted at by the one closed eye in the illustration.

Just as Water must flow out of its bed in order to cycle through nature and be renewed, emotion must be drawn from the well of Agana or our inner Water becomes stagnant, the valleys of our life become dry, and passion dies before it is born.

♥ deep unexpressed feeling

♥ emotions operating on a subconscious level

♥ potential for love, emotion, devotion

♥ the lonely, solitary heart

♥ desire

A♠
Terra Incognita

The World is always changing
  Ain't nothin' stays the same
  Come win or lose, tomorrow
  We begin another game.

Dame Fortuna's fickle finger
  Your cards will rearrange
  So there's nothin' you can count on
  Except that things will change.
                              —CJF

This card has long been referred to as the Papa Ace or the Death Ace and has become a source of superstitious fear for many. It seems even the casual card player senses the mystical power expressed by the Ace of Spades. This is *Terra Incognita*, meaning Hidden Earth. It is the form beneath the form, the skull beneath the skin, the truth concealed by the mask. The earthly form of all things will eventually pass, but along with this passing lies the potential for the re-creation, just as rotting Earth becomes fertile soil for new growth.

The stripping away of what is familiar can be a fearsome prospect. The appearance of this Ace warns us not to rely solely on the forms of this Earth, which are indeed castles of sand. We must find footing in other realms as well (represented by the three other suits) in order to walk through the doorway of change that is the Ace of Spades.

♠ something concealed, secrets

♠ change, a threshold

♠ death

♠ potential for re-creation

THE TWOS

CARDS BEARING THIS NUMBER PRESENT AN INTERESTING DYNAMIC. As next in line after the Ace, or One, the Deuces symbolize the first exploration outside of the self, outside of the singular aspect exemplified by the Ace. The concept here is self and other, or "How do I relate in the most basic way to the world outside myself?"

When taken in a positive, growth-oriented way, these cards involve opportunities for cooperation, partnership, and harmonious co-existence. When taken in a less than positive way, the Two becomes a field for opposition where differences are magnified and feelings of division and conflict take root.

2♦
The Rivals

Look carefully at the illustration on this card and behold the meeting of polarities. The bald-headed old man is as the sun, sinking into his bed of Earth as the last moments of daylight give way to the approaching darkness. The prowling night is personified as a young female perched on a bed of sky, ready to take her turn as ruler of the heavens. Sun-Moon. Light-Dark. Age-Youth. Earth-Sky. Male-Female.

Just as the struggle between light and dark gives rise to exceptional celestial events, a good rivalry or "clash" within our own lives can create a needed spark, the push that brings out our personal best, the motivation to reach for and achieve our highest potentials. When you see the 2 of Diamonds, ask yourself, "What is in competition in my life?" and "What potential can it bring out in me?"

♦ a rivalry

♦ a competition for attention or recognition

♦ polarities, friction

♦ a dynamic or financial partnership

♦ motivation to strive for your best

2♣
The Friends

Here we see a quiet, solitary figure, an enigmatic representation for a card called "The Friends." The geomantic pattern known as Conjunctio appears in a formation of twinkling stars, a figure associated with connection (see p. 149). But what is this person who sits alone connected to?

Quiet and solitude often allow a certain inner knowing to rise to the surface of our consciousness, bringing peace and an acceptance of the way things are. With this card, the Deuce energy, which is typically so intense and emotionally charged, is lightened and lifted by the airy, detached nature of the Club suit. Relationships based on the 2 of Clubs possess an aloofness, a separateness. There is a recognition of the need for personal space.

♣ peace, acceptance

♣ aloofness, remoteness

♣ like-mindedness / friendship

♣ curiosity / mental attraction

2♥
The Lovers

With "The Lovers," two hearts are in relationship, tethered by the sweet and bitter cords of emotion. Initial attraction or infatuation is not enough to form a bond of love. Fibers must be spun with tender patience, commitment, and compassion.

Because this card is in the suit of Hearts, the nakedness pictured here is not about physical nudity but emotional nudity, emotional intensity. The masks are all gone. All of one's fears and vulnerabilities are brought to the surface. What we are talking about is relationship at the deepest level.

When interpreting this card in a reading, do not try to limit it to the male/female lover example. There are heartfelt entanglements of many kinds.

♥	lovers
♥	a heartfelt relationship
♥	the love / hate continuum
♥	to feel vulnerable, exposed
♥	a "bond" of love / a marriage

2♠

The Enemies

The Spade Suit, corresponding to the solid and dense Element of Earth, provides the most concrete and pronounced example of opposition and division within the Deuces. Like rock against rock, sword against sword, this card represents the ultimate clash: two energies equally pitted in strength and determination.

Conflict has many possible levels of manifestation, be it between nations, neighbors, or *within* the individual. Resolution is a difficult concept for The Enemies. Often there is the perception that one side or the other must win, must conquer the other. Carl Jung once said, "a true conflict is never resolvable on the same level where it is experienced." Cooperation and understanding are the lessons of the number Two.

♠ opposition

♠ division, conflict of interest

♠ inability to find resolution

♠ wars, disputes

♠ inner turmoil

♠ need for harmony, cooperation

THE THREES

WHEN REFLECTING ON THE MEANING OF ANY CARD of the number Three, it helps to visualize the vertical formation of suit signs as the three rungs of a ladder. Imagine that you are standing on this ladder, balanced on the middle rung, and faced with the option of ascending or descending. Until a step is taken, a commitment made one way or the other, you are neither here nor there, but simply betwixt.

When a Three appears, know that things are in flux, seeking stability. There is an opportunity, an option, a choice. Situations like this occur frequently in life and can be a source of anxiety or an opportunity to align ourselves more closely with our own personal goals. We need to be clear about what we want and where we are going. People with more than one of these cards in their reading have a tendency to fret over or avoid making decisions.

3 ◆
The Necklace

On a necklace, objects of value and brilliance are strung together, connected. The vertical formation of Diamonds on this card can be viewed in just such a way: as a pathway of radiant gems that join the higher to the lower. The 3 of Diamonds suggests an alignment of energies that creates something new, something vibrant and transformational. People possessing "The Necklace" have a calling, so to speak. They are messengers of light.

The card illustrates doves descending like messengers from above as things are taking shape out of smoke. Contemplate these images and you will gain much insight. Frequently a business venture or artistic endeavor of some kind is at hand. Questions to ask may be, "What inspires me at this time?" or, "What is it that wants to be expressed through me?" As with all cards of the number Three, opportunity knocks, but for a given time only. Will you choose to answer?

◆ talent, inspiration

◆ things taking shape, transforming

◆ business or financial opportunities

◆ craftsmanship / artistic expression

◆ a string of events / 3 is a charm

3♣
The Wish

Thought is creative and has influence even beyond what we are willing to admit to ourselves. Look into the eyes of the figure underneath the table and make no mistake. What are *you* creating with *your* thoughts? Is it what you *really* want? Do not underestimate the power of the mind. As the old saying goes, be careful what you wish for, it might come true!

Certainly the 3 of Clubs is a card of great magnitude. It signals an opportunity to set the course of things yet to be, along with a warning to guard closely the direction of your thoughts.

Knowledge of the future is really not so mysterious. You don't need a crystal ball or even a card reader to reveal it to you. The secret lies in knowing how to look inside your own head.

♣ the creative power of the mind / the power of manifestation

♣ thinking things over, considering options

♣ a need for mental clarity, clear decisions

♣ a warning to guard your thoughts

3♥
The Clutch

Here we have three hearts connected, three affections. Looking at the illustration, we see a triangle and inside of it a Heart torn, fragmented, like pieces of a puzzle. What will it take to put ourselves back together? Three is a difficult number when it comes to matters of the heart. It beckons a choice, a decision. We must ask what is truly nurturing us, truly serving our emotional needs, and what is just adding emotional drama to our lives. Paper flowers, paper hearts, paper kisses, paper wings, all of this, and many more things, can make us feel, but are they real? Valentines fade, but true love is embossed on the scrolls of eternity.

How long will you wait? What will it take to go beyond the door of torn affection? Who or what holds the key? Are you willing to take the risk, to pay the cost? This card represents a balancing act of the emotions few can pull off with success, although there are exceptions. Surrounding cards can help to clarify each 3 of Hearts situation. Keep in mind also that matters of the heart are not always just between people. There are passions of many kinds.

♥ emotional drama

♥ playing "both sides of the fence" emotionally

♥ indecision, vacillation of the affections

♥ three hearts connected

♥ an affair / jealousy

3♠
The Grave

Three of Spades
Dig a Grave
Take time to choose
Just what you save
If not useful
Why carry it?
You might as well
Bury it.
—Laddy LaDoux

The appearance of this card suggests that time has come for something to be buried, to take its rightful place in the past. There is a need to "take stock," and let what is gone be recognized as such. Forward movement is aided only by what is living and vibrant.

When thinking of this card, I imagine a landscape of gravestones, the somber tolling of a distant bell marking the passage of time. Glimpses of engravings upon the stones pass my view, telling of things past. Most buried here are intangible: memories and dreams, fond and feared, that finally found their resting ground. Some gravestones, however, tell of things more real. Like grave markers, the cards that surround the 3 of Spades in your layouts indicate the nature of what is in "The Grave."

♠ a time to "let go"

♠ a burial

♠ a past that no longer serves

♠ a burden being carried

THE FOURS

FOUR IS A NUMBER THAT LENDS ITSELF TO STRUCTURE, ORGANIZATION. Even our orientation in time and space rests within the confines of this number. The four directions of the compass guide us on our way through space and the seasonal cycle of Four tells us where we are in time. Of course, let us not forget that the playing deck, too, has its basis in Four, with the Diamonds, Clubs, Hearts, and Spades.

In this system of card reading, each card in Four represents one of the four cardinal "winds": North, South, East, or West. As in ancient folklore, each wind possesses its own temperament or "mood." The suit signs on each of these cards can be seen as fence posts, outlining a playing field wherein events unfold according to the disposition of the wind that governs it.

More than one of these cards in any given spread is likely to indicate scattered energies, as currents blowing in different directions. Disorganization and carelessness are the potential pitfalls of the Fours, while organization and completion are the lessons.

4♦
The South Wind

The 4 of Diamonds introduces an impish dimension into our menagerie of card images. South is personified as the naughty bluster, the wind that takes pleasure in mischief and mayhem. You've seen him at work before, blowing the newly washed laundry off the clothesline or kicking up a cloud of blinding dust. This is the Dennis the Menace of the playing deck. Deals that seemed a sure thing suddenly go amiss, lines get crossed, and confusion and misunderstanding abound. When you see the 4 of Diamonds, plan on the unplanned.

♦ disturbances, unplanned circumstance

♦ confusion, misunderstanding

♦ a sense of humor, a joke

♦ the direction of South

SOUTH WIND

4♣
The East Wind

In Greek mythology it is written that East was the wind Zeus would hardly ever call upon to help him in his deeds, its forces being slower and weaker than the other winds. When you see this card, the mood is right for contemplation and thoughtful preparation. Forget about haste or making sudden decisions.

When I look at the face illustrated on the 4 of Clubs, I sometimes feel as though I am looking at the face of Grandfather Time himself, a venerable old soul complete with arthritic joints and a cane. There is no way you're going to get him to speed things up. No, he is just going to take his sweet time and things will get done when they get done. Remember, the most precious things in life often take a while to grow and develop. Patience is the lesson of this Four.

♣ slow and deliberate action

♣ careful thinking, turning something over in one's mind

♣ waiting for events to unfold

♣ things that occur over a long period of time

♣ a weak energy

♣ the direction of East

EAST WIND

CJF 99

4♥
The West Wind

The West Wind emanates an atmosphere of compassion and warmth. Like the breezes of Spring that carry the intoxicating fragrances of tender buds, this wind of the Heart suit has a gentle persuasion, lifting spirits and inviting us to put worry and conflict aside.

As westerly currents pass over the fields, flowers nod their heads gently in turn and grasses softly sway in a symphony of quiet agreement. The mood here is understanding. Under the influence of this card, opposing sides discover common ground, and lovers find comfort in each other's arms.

♥ a mood of harmony

♥ agreement

♥ understanding, peace

♥ acceptance

♥ love and tenderness

♥ the direction of West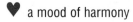

WEST WIND   CJF '99

4♠
The North Wind

This card represents an environment that is charged with strong dynamic force. Originating in cold harsh lands, this wind blows with raw and unsettling power. Legend tells that mares in the field with their backs turned to the North Wind would become impregnated by it. Indeed, this card often involves sexual energy or motivations. Like jumping on the back of a wild and bucking bronco, when you are dealing with the 4 of Spades, get ready for a ride you won't soon forget.

♠ a strong, unsettling energy

♠ raw power

♠ sexual motivations

♠ hardship, challenge

♠ the need to seek protection

♠ the direction of North

NORTH WIND   CJF '99

THE FIVES

IT'S BEEN TOLD THAT IN TIMES OF OLD, outcasts of society, such as thieves and those suspected of practicing magic, were buried outside of town where two roads crossed one another. This was done to confuse the spirit of the deceased, lest it entertain any ideas of heading back to its regular stomping grounds.

Looking at the suit symbols on the Fives, it is easy to see the outline of two roads as they cross one another, forming an X. The middle pip is as a traveler faced with a choice. Cards in Five commonly point to confusion brought about by newfound freedom or options. Often people will wander down one road, so to speak, then turn around and try another, ultimately going nowhere.

Fives are, more often than not, difficult cards. At their worst they represent a trap, usually of the person's own making. At best, they indicate options and influx of new energy, new possibilities and *change*.

5♦
Peddler's Ace

Curiously referred to centuries ago as the Peddler's Ace, the 5 of Diamonds signals caution and a warning to think clearly before entering into "deals" or transactions. Our daily lives are filled with transactions and exchanges of all kinds. Every relationship is made of give and take. When you see this card, it is valuable to ask, "What am I giving and what am I getting in my life? What is being bargained for?"

The Five of Diamonds
Is called the Peddler's Ace
And says in simple language
Beware the marketplace.
"I have all your heart's desires,"
You'll hear the peddler cry
But in fact he's selling humbug
And that's all your dollars buy.
     —CJF

As with any Five, it is wise not to act on impulse. Know that time is on your side. A little self-restraint in the face of temptation can help to clarify your options. The peddler usually has something fishy up his sleeve. Because this particular Five is in the suit of Diamonds, be especially careful of finances or dealings that may leave you with empty pockets, wondering what you really got in return.

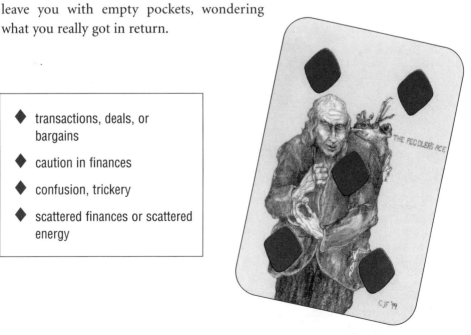

- ♦ transactions, deals, or bargains
- ♦ caution in finances
- ♦ confusion, trickery
- ♦ scattered finances or scattered energy

5♣
Wind Cape

The meaning of this card is depicted in an allegorical way in the story that follows. In it the powers of the mind can be likened to the tumultuous winds that possess poor Dumlin's cloak. Remember that Air is the Element of Clubs. With this card, ideas, plans, and dreams are "blowing" in every direction.

It is helpful when thinking of the 5 of Clubs to imagine yourself standing in the center of the card itself, in the position of the middle Club. The four surrounding Clubs are the four winds, each with its own direction and agenda. Certainly the whims of thought make a difficult master. The mind quickly becomes a trap, and confusion keeps the key just outside our reach.

♣ a mind that is going in every direction / mental confusion

♣ loss of memory

♣ to be "filled" with ideas and opinions

♣ surprising realizations, new ideas

♣ an over-inflated opinion of oneself

THE WIND CLOAK: *A Story*

It is said that in ancient times, Aeolus, God of the Winds, held his blustery progeny within himself, so that he would bellow and swell like a disheveled thundercloud when he walked the heavens. However, according to the Aeolians (his legendary descendants who once populated ancient Thessaly), Aeolus wore a cloak close about himself and it was in this cloak that he kept his unruly children, the Winds.

We find no further mention of Aeolus' cloak until the second century A.D., when Plethino, a minor neoplatonist writer, makes mention in his commentaries on the ancient myths that "Aeolus had a cape that took life unto itself spirited by the four Winds."

All of this is only of passing interest until we come to the fifteenth century and a story related in the Heidelberg Chronicles compiled by C. Agrippa. Here we are told of one Albertus Dumlin (1384-1437), a frustrated alchemist who lived in Rotterdam. Having exhausted his meager resources searching for the secret by which metals could be transmuted, Dumlin was about to sell his old cloak for a much needed dram of raven's blood when it suddenly inflated, seemingly caught by a gust of air. This proved to be exceedingly odd since Dumlin was then standing at the back of an apothecary shop where, judging from a heavy encrustment of dust that covered every crevice, no air had moved in at least twenty years.

Now here was a man of science, a reasonable, methodical man whose methods rigidly adhered to laws established by cause and effect. As there was, in this instance, no discernable cause for the afflatus that momentarily possessed his old and somewhat bedraggled cape, Dumlin was dumbfounded. Rather than sell the cloak, as he had intended, he exchanged his linen ruff, which was in much better condition, for the dram of raven's blood and hastily went home to ponder nature's anomalies. For hours Dumlin experimented— sprinkling small amounts of the dried blood on both shoulders, dissolving the powder in arsenic and applying it wet over the cloak's lining, steaming the blood in various solutions and applying it as a vapor up his sleeves—but nothing he tried produced the desired effect, i.e., the afflatus of his cape.

Exhausted and disheartened, a perplexed Dumlin finally prepared to retire, intent upon continuing his experiments afresh the next morning when, touching his shoulder to disrobe, the cloak inexplicably inflated as if taken by a breath of wind. This time it swirled more vigorously than before and only stopped after some moments. Dumlin felt a tingle up his humped spine. Once more he touched his shoulder and the cloak again leaped to life, nearly knocking him off his feet. Obviously, thought Dumlin, the old cloak he had found in a pile of rags just the day before had magical powers.

At ten o'clock the next morning he marched into Sun Dial Square in the heart of town and announced proudly before a curious crowd that he, Albertus Dumlin, scholar of universal knowledge, alchemist, physicist, mathematician, geographer, and philosopher, held in his cape the Four Winds, which he would harness like horses for the benefit of all mankind. Whereupon, with a grand gesture, he touched his shoulder and the cloak responded, swirling up as a thing possessed, lifting Dumlin a good two feet off the ground before sweeping him head over heels past the crowd and down the street.

In silent amazement, everyone watched as poor Dumlin was propelled about like a leaf in a storm until finally, kicking and screaming, he sailed into the canal and presumably drowned. Our alchemist was never seen again. But his cloak? Well, it was pulled out of the water several miles down river by a fisherman and hung in the sun to dry.

—CJF

5♥
Fata Morgana

The words Fata Morgana come from the Arthurian Tales and literally mean the spell of Morgana. And who is Morgana? Why, none other than the Spade Queen herself—the legendary sorceress of the pack.[2] A casual glance in the direction of this enchantress poised in the lake would cause many a heart to flutter. But take a second, more careful look and behold the reflection of a hag.

Over the course of time, many illusions (fata) will be cast upon the waters of our emotions, but these are only shadow images, reflections lacking depth. How easy it is for the quivering, uncertain heart to be led astray. Can one be still enough to find one's center, to see beyond the clashing of dreams, to penetrate the surface of what is being shown?

♥ an illusion, a fantasy

♥ a restless heart

♥ a "change of heart"

♥ an allurement or attraction

♥ emotion lacking depth

[2] The influence of the Spade Queen within the Hearts demonstrates how card energies can overlap suit boundaries. Other more obvious examples of this can be found in the Six of Clubs, the Jack of Clubs, and the King of Diamonds.

5♠
Circle of Crows

When giving readings that involve this card, I get the image of a group of cawing crows, circling low overhead against a still, grey sky. There is something unsettling, even haunting about their presence. One feels trapped, encircled. The way out is unclear.

More than any other Five, the "Circle of Crows" denotes a feeling of being at a crossroads, with no one road appearing any more promising than another. Because this is a card in the Spade suit, here we are talking about issues like work or housing or our physical well-being. Often present is a high degree of dissatisfaction or frustration, accompanied by skepticism or fear. If one has religious beliefs or trust in a higher power, now is the time to call on it. In a larger spread, surrounding cards can help illuminate what lies ahead should one so choose a particular direction.

♠ to feel trapped or ganged up on

♠ uncertainty, frustration

♠ dismal prospects / an unsatisfying job

♠ constriction, fear of change

♠ feeling a victim

THE SIXES

LOOKING AT THE SIXES IN *THE PICTURE BOOK OF ANA CORTEZ*, notice they are depicted as structures, and what is a structure but a place to hold our experiences? As such, cards of this number convey the feeling of being sheltered. They are places of comfort and rest. The arrangement of suit symbols reflects this. It outlines a pathway, a little stretch of open road without blockage or disturbance. This is a key observation in understanding the nature of these cards. When Sixes are present in a reading, you find harmony and freedom from conflict or worry.

Further insight can be gained into the number Six by observing it within the natural order. Six is an even number, sandwiched between Five and Seven. Five suggests change and Seven brings the challenge of the sword. Accordingly, we can rightly view the Six as a time to "breathe easy" between more difficult situations, a time to gather one's resources and energy before going out to "face the world" again.

Of course, each step on the pathway of numbers has lessons to bestow and pitfalls to beware, and Six is no exception. The negative side arises when we use this place of retreat to hide from personal challenges. Many Sixes in a reading typically indicate stagnancy, an avoidance of those things that must be faced in order to grow.

6♦

The Tower

Ascending the spiral of stairs within The Tower, a changing sensation sets in. One gets the increasing feeling of being elevated. Arriving at the top and gazing out, an incredible expanse of land and sky opens up before you. You see now what you could not from the ground. Along with such far-reaching vision comes a feeling of protection and peace. Nothing here will come by surprise. All things can be known beforehand. But in this lofty place where movement is limited to simply up or down, isolation and boredom quickly embrace. Although offering security and predictability, it is these same qualities that, in time, can transform The Tower into a prison.

- ♦ a vantage point, vision
- ♦ security, protection, especially regarding finances
- ♦ a bank
- ♦ predictability, monotony
- ♦ isolation, confinement
- ♦ a prison
- ♦ to be elevated or looked up to / recognition, fame

6♣

The Bridge

Less a place than a process, a bridge is a fascinating structure unlike any other. "Bridging" two otherwise disconnected places, this card represents safe crossing over troubled waters. Bridges of the inner world arise as we are ready to transcend obstacles, the hurts and the fears that have prevented us from moving on in our lives. Newfound perspectives and newfound hopes form the bricks that pave the passage.

Remember that when on a bridge one can travel in either direction. What awaits on different shores presents an interesting prospect: future or past. Within a spread, cards laid out on the left and right of the 6 of Clubs can complete a landscape wherein further insights can be revealed (*see The Bridge Layout*, p. 176).

♣ moving onward to a new place in your life

♣ new perspectives

♣ surmounting, overcoming obstacles

♣ finding peace of mind

♣ "bridging" future and past / remembering

♣ a message or messenger

6♥
The Castle

The 6 of Hearts is the fortress of our emotions, the walls that shelter our most intimate and personal lives. More often than not, this card represents the home. When the long day is over, when we've had enough and need a place to rest, The Castle offers the comfort of the familiar. Here we can let down our defenses and "be ourselves." In this place we find connection to our roots, our family and loved ones. It is where our earliest memories are born. Within The Castle lies the key to our subconscious and the emotional memories that have patterned our lives.

♥ the home

♥ emotional harmony, emotional comfort

♥ a place of the heart, where your heart is

♥ a hospital or place of healing

♥ nostalgia or sentimentality

♥ roots and family

6♠

The Ruin

On a high deserted plain, covered with snow and all the stillness of winter, The Ruin stands. This solitary monument of the past appears to remind us that what once was is no more. Within its hollow semblance, memories echo amongst the falling debris and cold whispers of wind. Though time marches on, the past lingers within us, often dictating the present. Old walls eventually crumble, yet provide bricks that can be used to lay new foundations. With this card, Winter comes like sleep, putting all to rest in preparation for the renewal of Spring.

♠ a lingering past

♠ something that has been neglected or destroyed

♠ form without substance or life

♠ a past that can provide lessons for the future

♠ hibernation or rest, winter

THE SEVENS

MANY MYSTICAL TRADITIONS ATTRIBUTE THE NUMBER SEVEN with great spiritual significance. Looking at the formation of pips, we see a continuation of the pathway outlined by the Sixes, but with the appearance of an obstacle, a "stone in the road," so to speak. With these cards, a challenge is being presented along with the forced need to turn inward and contemplate life strategies.

In *The Picture Book of Ana Cortez*, the Sevens are symbolized as swords, implements well suited for challenge. A sword calls forth our greatest resources, our greatest powers of focus and responsibility. As these cards appear in a reading, the *inner* world is under examination.

The number Seven stands perfectly in the middle of each 13-card suit, making these the only cards that are neither high nor low. Just as all swords have two edges, when manifesting the Seven we look out and choose between the higher and the lower, between evolution and involution, depending on which side of the blade is used: constructive or destructive.

It is fascinating to notice that the pips on a Seven form two perfect and distinct geomantic figures, depending on the direction the card is viewed (see *The Figures*, p. 145). From one side, the beneficent figure of Albus appears (symbolizing good beginnings, intelligence, experience) and from the other, the potentially disastrous figure of Rubeus rears its head (a warning to stop, violence, even blood). Two more perfect correspondences could hardly be found for the choices and potential consequences represented by these cards.

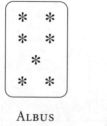

ALBUS

RUBEUS

7 ♦

Sword of Truth

As explained, the number Seven deals with the inner world, not the outer. Because of this, the usual monetary associations of the Diamond suit take an interesting twist in Seven. This card is about the riches of the inner life, or spiritual cash as opposed to the green stuff.

The Sword of Truth is just what it says, a means of discerning truth. I picture the blade of this sword cutting through and banishing fog—the fog of false thinking, of false perception. Once clouds are cleared, the light of truth shines through unobstructed.

Living this virtue takes courage, perseverance, and a willingness to see things as they really are. Like all cards of the sword, it represents a gift, a power, but one that must be prudently applied. Carelessly used, truth can injure. People are not always prepared for it. As the saying goes, "All things their time and place," and truth is no exception.

Knowledge all our teachers teach
  As they were taught before
  To use it we must always reach
  Beyond the knowledge door.

Experience life's path to light
  Ability to see
  Wisdom will unveil your sight
  Use it and be free.
                                    —Laddy LaDoux

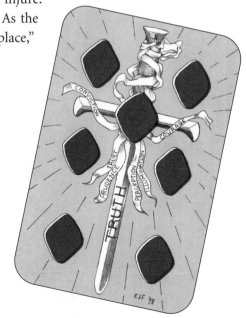

♦ the truth

♦ living rightly or living truth

♦ teaching, illumination

♦ a call for prudence, wisdom

7♣

Sword of Enchantment

The appearance of this card within a reading signals the presence of something very special. A shining, mystical gift from the realm of Ethra is at hand and magic is afoot! Less a "sword" than the other cards in Seven, perhaps it is better conceptualized as a key. With the blessings of this Seven tucked into your pocket, "unexplainable" events come into being. Opportunities "magically" present themselves, the right person "coincidentally" happens to be at the right place at the right time, etc. In short, doors once closed can be opened with the key that is the 7 of Clubs. The bearer of this card is a walking magnet, directing spiritual traffic even without conscious intention.

As with all Sevens, a certain responsibility is needed. What is projected has the predictable tendency to come full circle. Remember when reading this card that Clubs is the suit that deals with what a person thinks. Positive thoughts attract positive circumstance at the moment we need it most. Negative thinking draws only dark clouds, creating difficulties, "accidents," and the like.

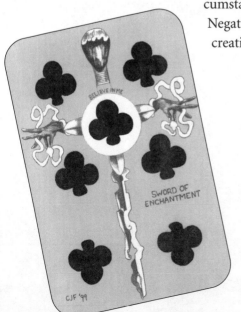

- ♣ the power of thought as it effects reality
- ♣ coincidences, synchronicity
- ♣ magic, enchantment
- ♣ belief in the unseen

7♥

Sword of Healing

On this card you can see the blade of a sword emerging from the depths of the Water, the flowing Element of life and love. As with all Sevens, it represents a gift, a charm, and power to be coveted yet strictly revered. When the "Sword

Who can say what healing is?
Perhaps a path to peace
But first you must look to yourself
If you want to find release.
                    —Laddy LaDoux

of Healing" reveals itself within a spread, a challenge of love and/or healing is at hand. Directed properly, the cooling, nourishing Waters represented by Hearts are brought to cleanse and restore sickened body and saddened soul. But be forewarned! Sweet medicine turns to vile poison by careless use of this sword. The blade that heals becomes the knife that injures, inflicting sickness and the wounds of passion. Interpretive techniques discussed later in the text will help you decide which meanings apply in a given instance.

♥ the power of healing, the power of love

♥ forgiveness

♥ infliction of sickness, suffering

♥ a surgeon's blade

7♠

Sword of Destruction

It is important here to realize that destruction can be not only a harmful force, but also a helpful force, necessary for a strong and productive life. The blade of the 7 of Spades symbolizes an ability to cut away those things that no longer serve, like "cutting off" a bad relationship or a nasty habit. Much as a gardener prunes the limbs that are not producing growth, we, too, can prune to strengthen what is healthy and vital in our lives.

This is of course the positive application, existing beside a potentially dangerous one. Look at the illustration on this card and note the chain attached to the handle of the sword, a very short and very strong chain, along with the curious figures cuddling the sword's deadly edges. Why hug up to such a thing? Destruction has an energy that is seductive. It is associated with power. As a society we are fascinated by it. The violence in our media testifies to this.

Beware this sword. Exercise the utmost care. When not thoughtfully aimed, the power represented produces senseless destruction, loss, and grief.

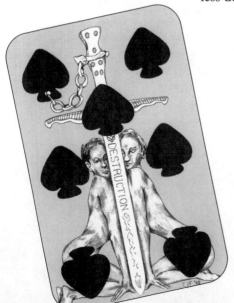

♠ the ability to cut off or let go of those things that do not serve

♠ the need to exercise control, discipline

♠ the power to do harm

♠ destruction

THE EIGHTS

AS WITH ALL PIPS CARDS (Ace through Nine), a visual clue is provided in the arrangement of suit signs. On the Eights, you have a tightly knit formation, a fortified group of symbols.

In the succession of numbers, Eight follows Seven. It is the outcropping of challenges faced by cards of the sword. In Eight, we must live with the results, good or bad, accumulated over the course of time, depending on how we have handled the challenges in our lives, on choices and sacrifices made or not made.

At best, these cards represent success, achievement, and the ability to bask in the rewards of one's labors. At worst, the Eight symbolizes the reaping of a bitter feast, the fruition of poor choices and the misfortune thereof. A strong emphasis on cards of this number within a given layout indicates a person who is results-oriented with materialistic tendencies.

```
*    *
   *
*    *
   *
*    *
```

8 ◆

The House of Good Fortune

This card heralds the presence of good fortune and success. Seeds once planted have finally come to fruition and it is time to reap the harvest (remember, Diamonds is the suit of Autumn). Make plans now for expansion. Check to see if goals have been clearly defined. Refuse to accept limitations of the past. Push yourself, test your boundaries, but avoid the pitfall of becoming overly ambitious or power hungry. Remain humble.

Many helpful correspondences for this card can be gleaned from the symbolism hinted at by the lion's head pictured on the door. Though largely solitary, lions achieve their greatest success in groups—especially when hunting. In human terms, hunting corresponds to the pursuit of a goal. Lions are courageous, self-assured creatures. They take their victories in stride, exuding a radiant yet calm dominion over their surroundings. With the 8 of Diamonds, there is incredible strength, an inner Fire that burns. Shoulders are broad and there is bounty enough to share.

- ◆ good luck / good fortune
- ◆ success in groups, team activity
- ◆ prosperity, expansion
- ◆ good timing
- ◆ ambition / materialism
- ◆ demand for recognition, power

8♣
The Scales

There is something about the 8 of Clubs that borders on the holy. The window could be part of a church or monastery. The view itself conveys a feeling of peace, loftiness.

Clouds are an archetypal symbol for thoughts or ideas. Too many thoughts clutter our ability to think clearly, just as too many clouds obscure vision. On this card, we see that there is space enough for movement, for light.

The scale, of course, pertains to balance, and here we are talking about balance as it relates to the mind. When "The Scales" appears in a reading, it is time to throw away biased or negative thought patterns, time to discover a more enlightened way of looking at things. Like the clouds that hover high above the earth's surface, we can raise our thoughts to a new level, looking beyond what our eyes perceive, beyond our current reality.

♣ mental abilities / mental balance

♣ clarity / peace / transcendence

♣ justice / right decision

♣ minds joining together / mental support

♣ belief systems / ideologies

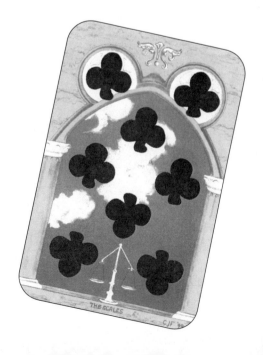

8♥

The Garden

A garden is often used as a metaphor for life. What would the garden of *your* life look like? Picture it in your mind. This card symbolizes a garden in Spring (the season corresponding to the Heart suit). The Hearts allude to the kind of labors that make this metaphorical garden grow: those of love.

Picture now a landscape of meandering walkways, lined with flowers of vivid color and radiant beauty. Exotic fragrances fill the damp air, tantalizing the senses. Beneath a fine broad tree and camouflaged by its leaves a snake lies in repose, mystical guardian of all that surrounds, master of charm and power. Traversing this exquisite garden, will you succumb to its sweet intoxication, like Dorothy who fell asleep in the field of poppies just before reaching the gates of Oz? With the 8 of Hearts, remember to keep your senses about you. There is much to be done in the garden of life.

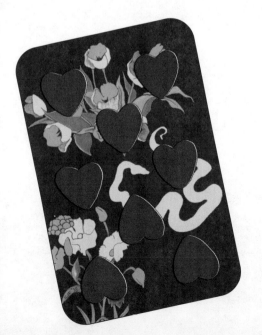

♥ labors of love

♥ loving support or a loving environment

♥ allurement of the senses

♥ beauty, charm

♥ temptation

8♠

Dating back to the time of Napoleon, the 8 of Spades was believed to be a card of ill omen; in fact, it was considered the unluckiest card in the deck. The dense field of Spade pips represents numerous obstacles and the fruition of "bad seeds." The meanings indicated here are fairly straightforward. The figure tied to the rock is in a rather helpless position and looking like somebody's lunch. The hourglass shows that time is up. Note that it is the opposite of the hourglass shown on the 8 of Diamonds, the card representing *good* fortune. One suggestion for someone receiving this card could be to simply hold off on plans until the timing is better, when obstacles have a chance to clear. To forge onward into the treacherous landscape that is The Field of Stones is likely to create further problems and is probably an impossible proposition to begin with.

♠ difficult karma

♠ numerous obstacles

♠ bad timing / bad luck

♠ time "run out"

♠ the need to wait, to rethink strategies

♠ a threatening group, an army

THE NINES

AFTER PASSING THROUGH THE EXPERIENCE of all other numbers, we arrive at Nine and find ourselves at the threshold of the court. Nine is the last pip in the playing deck, and the trials represented by these cards are in many ways our final trials.

The vibration of this number resonates with the vibration of each number that has come before it and holds a vision that is all encompassing. It is a full pendulum swing from the Ace, the singular voice at the opposite end of the spectrum. The calling for people faced with cards in Nine is indeed great, and success is measured by the degree of selfless humanitarian action. Motives stemming from selfishness always spell disaster.

Because of the finality these cards represent, Nines will frequently tell of endings in a reading. Something has entered its last stage. Divorce, for example, often appears as a Nine.

The idea of extremes is also commonly depicted by cards of this number. Numerologically speaking, no number possesses the magnitude that a Nine does, simply because all numbers, no matter how complex, are ultimately reduced to a single digit to receive their value. Nine is the max. Correspondingly, people who have Nines in their layout are the type who like to go about things in a full-tilt sort of way. Moderation is not their style. Along this same line, you will find that the meanings attributed to cards of this number are also quite extreme. The positive correspondences are among the most noble in the pack while the negatives sink to the very bottom of the bucket.

Because of their proximity to the court, the Nines have a very unique job in the playing deck, acting as a sort of passageway or bridge between the pips and the court. This means that in a reading, they will occasionally represent people themselves, a function usually reserved for cards of higher ranking. This metamorphic ability is reflected in the card illustrations with two of the Nines depicted as people. When these cards do symbolize a person, it is typically a youth, though more often than not the Nines operate as the pips they are, illuminating circumstances, experiences, or events.

Similar to other odd-numbered cards, the configuration of suit signs outlines a pathway with an obstacle placed in the center. Depending on the individual, the trials represented will serve either as stepping stones or stumbling blocks.

9♦

Sir Gawain, the quintessential "Knight in Shining Armor," exemplifies the attributes of courage and uncompromising dedication to truth and service. Touted in tales of old as a solar hero, his strength reputedly increased with the rising sun, peaked at midday, and waned with the fading light. As such, this card symbolizes a changing dynamic, an energy that is here and then gone, an interest that peaks and then wanes. Ever wandering, Gawain comes galloping in on his trusty steed, just in time to save the day. Lingering no longer than it takes to right the wrong, to heed the call of duty, he rides off once more, into the setting sun.

For those manifesting this card there is always the promise of another challenge, another adventure. There is a need to "do battle" for the common good. Personal motivations are rejected as inferior to those that serve a broader purpose.

♦ devotion to duty, service, humanitarian causes

♦ a helpful person, a protector

♦ one who is here and then gone

♦ an adventure seeker

♦ a climax of energy followed by a waning of energy

9♣

Galahad

Among the legendary knights of the Round Table, Galahad is credited with finding the Grail, the only champion pure enough and devoted enough to pull off the "impossible." As with all Nines, it is a difficult card, presenting a test. Often there is a very idealistic vision being represented. With such high aspirations, it is easy for many to become disconnected from reality. Although Galahad's vision was certainly extreme, he was able to keep his focus and make great personal sacrifice in order to attain it.

When we take it in our head
To make alive a dream
Anything is possible
But never as it seems.

Being so far from the ground
Our head can become lost
Step one, step two
You must stay true
For always there is a cost.
　　　　　—Laddy LaDoux

Appropriate questions may be, "What is my goal, my dream?" and, "What are the sacrifices I must make in order to turn it into a reality?" then, "Am I willing to make those sacrifices?"

♣ idealism

♣ lofty visions or goals

♣ one on a search, on a mission

♣ personal sacrifice

♣ purity, piousness

♣ a miracle

GALAHAD

9♥
Gilles de Rais

A prominent figure in fifteenth century France, Gilles de Rais (pronounced Jeel duh Ray) was a man of tremendous stature and nobility. But as time wore on, Gilles' motives became increasingly self-serving. Much as Water that rises to become a flood, his decadent behavior swelled out of control, wreaking havoc for everyone and everything.

As the overflowing Hearts depicted on the card suggest, this Nine represents excesses of emotion. Those expressing its energy can easily feel "swept away" by the sheer intensity of their own sensitivities, giving rise to fears, insecurities, and compulsive behaviors.

A positive expression for this card can be found when one remembers that the vibration of the number Nine is humanitarian. By taking an active concern for others, the extraordinary depth of feeling represented here can be channeled, like Water itself. The passion of the Heart suit becomes centered in *com*passion. Though exceptional, when the energy of this Nine is manifested in a truly selfless way, this can be one of the most positive cards in the deck.

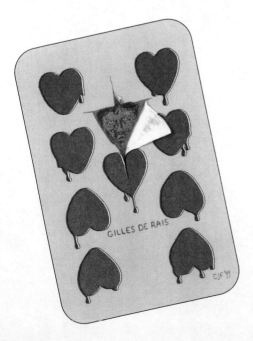

GILLES DE RAIS

♥ overwhelming emotion

♥ extremes of behavior, compulsiveness

♥ fears and insecurities

♥ suspicions / jealousy

♥ flowing tears / sorrow

♥ compassion / selfless caring for others

♥ humanitarian love

9♠
The Throne of Spiders

This Nine is heavy duty, indicating situations that have gotten way out of hand. Recall now that Earth is the Element corresponding to Spades. In Nine, earthly values, earthly concerns, or earthly addictions have become all consuming. Matter is winning the battle over spirit.

Spiders are nature's vampires, trapping and mummifying their prey with silky threads, then sucking to consume the precious life-giving forces. As graphic as this may seem, it is necessary to understand what is happening on an energetic level when this card appears in a reading. Something has become a Dracula, slowly extracting the enthusiasms, aspirations, and joy for living that feed the spirit, leaving only an earthly shell, a lost soul.

Remember always that no card is without hope. As human beings we are not victims. We are creatures of choice, though sometimes the choices are very difficult. When carrying our burdens involves the ultimate price, it is often better to "cut the load" than to be buried by it.

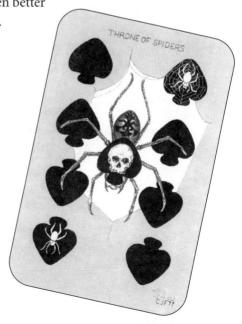

- ♠ an energy drain / a heavy burden
- ♠ overworking yourself
- ♠ addiction or co-dependence
- ♠ bad company / peers leading you in a poor direction
- ♠ a need to let go

INTRODUCING THE COURTS

TRAVERSING NOW BETWEEN THE NUMBERS Nine and Ten, we cross the border that separates the pips from the courts and enter royal territory. Here is where the hierarchy of the playing deck resides, cards commonly known as Kings, Queens, Jacks, and the less commonly known Ladies.

In the early history of playing cards, the French became fond of naming cards within the court, a practice they carry on to this day. Popular personalities existing in the culture at different periods, such as political figures or heroes and heroines from legends and myths, would make their way into the deck. The courts came to be associated with certain personalities, giving them depth of meaning.

Like this tradition, the courts presented in this book each have a name and personality. Some come from the French, but most have been newly fashioned to fit into the structure of the deck as it exists for card reading. They represent the people in our lives, the heroes and heroines of our own legends.

Now let's turn our attention to the look of the courts. People sometimes seem confused by the fact that *The Picture Book of Ana Cortez* features no card index, that is to say, no little K or Q or J in the corners. These corner markings are a relatively modern addition to playing cards (19th Century) added by cardmakers for the purpose of games: i.e., so you could hold a spread of cards in your hand and see what you have just by looking at the corners. In this deck, as in historical decks, you will need to look at the whole card in order to differentiate one from another. This should be no problem as spreads in card reading facilitate this. Kings and Queens, being of the highest rank, are portrayed very large, like a close-up photograph. Jacks and Ladies, on the other hand, are illustrated as if from farther away, making them full-figured, which means you see the whole person, head to foot. To further avert any confusion about which card is what, the courts in *The Picture Book* also feature their original number: Kings are thirteen, Queens are twelve, Jacks are eleven, and Ladies are ten. The numbers will also prove useful later on when you learn to supplement your readings with geomancy.

As you familiarize yourself with the personalities that make up the court, bear in mind that people take on different roles at different times in their lives. Card assignments must remain fluid. Maybe I am most similar to Morgana (the 12 of ♠) when I am at work but take on the characteristics of Livia (12 of ♦) when it comes to issues related to home. Viewed from the perspective of my parents, I remain forever a youth, probably expressed best by one of the Ladies (cards of the number Ten), for example. Depending on who is asking the question and which area of life is being represented, one and the same person can wear a variety of faces. Again, as always, count on the cards to lead you back to your own intuition.

THE LADIES

THE TENS, OR LADIES, AS THEY WILL BE REFERRED TO, are the first members that this approach to card reading includes within the court. Lady cards fit so well into the whole scheme of the deck. They restore balance to the male and female ratio of the court and provide a natural mate or counterpart for the Jack. When found alongside each other in a reading, Ladies and Jacks typically portray young couples or partnerships that are characterized by the nature of the suit (or suits) in which they appear. A Diamond Lady and Jack, for example, would be a dynamic, charismatic partnership that could be used to generate finances. A Club partnership would indicate shared intellectual interests, etc.

Historically, Lady cards were incorporated into the court to provide handmaidens for the Queens[3]. Truly, much insight can be gained into the individual character of each when one considers the personality and temperament of the Queen she must answer to: i.e., the Queen of her own suit. Generally speaking, the Ladies tend to be headstrong with an unquenchable thirst for independence. This is natural enough when you recall that the number on these cards is an extension of the number One.

In readings, Ladies can signify not only younger females but also older females who are younger in spirit. This could be a "young soul," or someone exploring a more youthful aspect of themselves. I commonly see Ladies represent older women who are embarking on something brand new, who are starting over in some capacity. The cards reflect what a person is projecting *energetically*.

[3] See *Book Two*, pgs. 218-219

10♦

Tendra

Tendra, the young and alluring female of the Diamond suit, certainly leads a charmed life. Lavished so completely with the family's wealth, what can money possibly buy her that she does not already have? Yet for all her possessions and advantages, Tendra is hardly one to be satisfied.

Thinking now of the Element associated with this card suit, much can be explained regarding this Lady's character. Fire contains a dynamic spirit that is ever hungry. It consumes. The more it is given, the more it needs. This is the aspect of Fire that illuminates so well the personality of Tendra. Like a flame, she draws in, seduces, and demands. Even people have become things to possess. Her name reminds me of the words tender and tendril, giving one the sense of a creeping, clutching vine. The head of Tendra's desired is severed and yet she clings, enamored most by what she cannot have.

♦ obsessive / clutching

♦ a young woman of financial advantage

♦ needy or demanding, spoiled

♦ willful, tenacious

♦ a youthful, fiery female

THE SEVERED HEAD: *A Story*

Long ago, there lived near Tropalo in old Tusan twin brothers so alike in their physical being few could tell them apart except when they spoke, for one had the gift of words and the other only an idiot's babble. Now Elloot's skill with languages and his grasp of reason and philosophy were well beyond his years, so all who heard him speak considered him very wise. On the other hand, although an accomplished mime who could play with spoons and make wondrous noises, his brother Sooloot spoke imperfectly, and with great difficulty might express only the simplest thought. Mostly he babbled incoherently and was therefore considered an idiot. Yet, the two brothers were inseparable, and one was never seen without the other.

It came to pass that the King's daughter, Tendra, was entranced by Elloot's lovely language and fell in love with him. The King was also much impressed by Elloot, dubbing him Elloot the Wise. However, unable to countenance Sooloot, who seemed a monstrosity at best, the King offered his daughter's hand only if Elloot would forever part company with his brother. This Elloot forthrightly refused to do.

Now, Tendra grew much distressed, and determined she would finally separate the brothers by having Sooloot slain. That night, her manservant went secretly to Elloot's chamber and, finding the room in darkness with both brothers asleep—one in a proper bed and the other curled on the floor—he slew the brother sleeping on the floor, thinking him to be the idiot, Sooloot.

When her servant returned with Sooloot's severed head, Tendra received it with shocked apprehension and instinctively kissed its dead lips, for the visage looked strikingly like that of the brother she loved. Indeed, there was never any way of knowing whether Elloot or Sooloot had been slain, for the surviving twin from that time on never spoke or uttered a sound.

—CJF

10♣

Fortuna

Of airy nature, Fortuna is governed by no one and nothing save for the soul of the merry little breeze abiding within her. Try to grasp her and she will slip through your fingers. Try to predict her and you may as well try to chart a course for Lady Luck herself. Fortuna is here and gone, then back again tomorrow, or is it next week? No matter, this damsel of breezes will amuse and delight. A lighthearted lass, curious and clever-tongued, she knows how to get herself in and out of a jam, much as a cat possessing nine lives. I believe it was Fortuna who authored the phrase, "It is a woman's prerogative to change her mind," and this Fortuna will do. You can count on it.

♣ fickle or flighty, inconstant

♣ versatile, curious

♣ clever

♣ lighthearted

♣ a performer / actor or actress, dancer

10♥

Allegra

Allegra, Hearts' Lady of Romance
  Her cup is filled with wine that's rich,
Like pleasant circumstance.
But if you sip, then ask yourself
  Is it happiness you're drinking?
  Or just a moment's tender whim
  In need of your clear thinking?

—AC

As the youngest of the Heart suit family, Allegra embodies a youthful enthusiasm and naiveté in regard to her realm of emotion. We see from the card that her eyes are blinded—a symbol of logic lost, vision sacrificed for the cause of the beating heart. Following only the compass of her own emotions, boldly does this wild huntress pursue the objects of her affections. The journey for Allegra is filled with risk, the outcome far from certain, but predictability is not what she seeks. Excitement and desire feed this Lady's spirit.

As always, when attempting to penetrate the essential meaning of a card, it is helpful to consider the Element associated with its suit. In the given instance, we must relate with Water. Like her Element, Allegra is subject to fluctuations and the ever-changing tides of joy and sorrow, passion and pain.

♥ passionate, romantic

♥ young at heart

♥ vulnerable

♥ daring, risk-taking

♥ impulsive

♥ emotional, moody

10♠

Terrene

Terrene can perhaps be best conceptualized as the serving girl. Reflect on the fact that Morgana is the Queen she must answer to, the unsympathetic disciplinarian of the pack. I often think of this card as a kind of Cinderella figure catering to the demands of the stepmother. Never seeming to tire, Terrene tends her realm in Earth, nurturing, sustaining. Though modest, this Lady projects an inner radiance palpable to all. When thinking of the energy of this card, I imagine myself as an infant, wrapped in the reassuring arms of Terrene, like arms of the Earth. I am comforted, protected. I want for nothing.

Among the typically rather unstable, impulse-driven personalities represented by the Ladies, Terrene is certainly the most "grounded." She is generally a positive card, a real treasure amidst the characteristically dark and difficult Spade suit. Many aspects of the "natural female" are symbolized here, including the wisdom of the body and one's own instincts, the need for touch, and the sensual experience of the self.

♠ earthy, grounded

♠ serving or subservient

♠ melancholic

♠ nurturing, protecting

♠ practical

♠ meek or modest

♠ tactile / sensual

THE JACKS

ELEVEN IS THE NUMBER GIVEN TO THE FIRST MALE CARDS within the court, commonly referred to as Jacks. This is a notoriously rascally bunch. Fun loving and high-spirited, Jacks possess an undeniable appeal. They are adventurous, and, like the Lady cards, strongly driven toward independence.

Generally speaking, Jacks take responsibility for no one save themselves and the King or Queen to whom they must be accountable. In a layout, these cards take on more upstanding characteristics in the presence of higher authority. It's as if Mom and Dad are watching their behavior.

Jacks commonly represent younger men; however, they can represent an older man who is playing out his younger self, displaying his less mature personality traits in whatever situation is being depicted in the reading.

11 ♦

Dango

As the end of the evening draws near, a hush sweeps over the crowd and brilliant light flashes high in the darkened arena. From the ground below, Dango appears not as a man, but a glittering white star in a circus tent sky. With mouths agape, the mystified crowd looks on as this master showman moves fearlessly across the blazing aerial wire.

This is a knave who knows not he is a knave. He is bigger than life, constantly walking the line between fantasy and reality, between possible and impossible. This card often represents someone who is pushing the limit in some way, performing a balancing act of sorts, going on faith, or working under intense pressure.

In questions of relationship, it is good to recognize that this is a guy who lives at the center of his own universe. Compelling and dynamic, Dango is dazzling, but mostly to himself. As part of the suit associated with the Element of Fire, he can be compared to the flickering flame of a candle. Try to catch hold of him and he will disappear from sight, leaving only a burn to remember him by. Dango prizes freedom above all other possessions and there is little he will not sacrifice for it.

- ♦ dramatic, a showman
- ♦ courageous or daring
- ♦ performing under pressure
- ♦ vain or self-interested
- ♦ freedom-loving

11♣

Lancelot du Lac

An enduring figure in French playing card history, Lancelot's name appears on the Jack of Clubs in decks as early as the fifteenth century and as late as the mid-nineteenth century. First written of more than eight hundred years ago, tales of Lancelot's remarkable adventures have an enduring magnetism. But what is it that sets him apart from his fellow knights? Legend tells that upon the death of his mother, the infant Lancelot was taken from his cradle to be raised in "a land under waves" by the Lady du Lac (Lady of the Lake), who bestowed upon him magical powers and christened him Lancelot "du Lac." When finally released by his fairy mother eighteen years later, Lancelot emerges from the Water essentially reborn, no longer a man but an extraordinary being. He encompasses both the male (the rational, conscious realm into which he was born) and the female (the intuitive, unconscious realm where he was raised), providing a unique link between the Club and Heart suits.

LANCELOT DU LAC

- ♣ extraordinary and varied abilities
- ♣ an androgynous male/female quality
- ♣ artistic
- ♣ spiritual
- ♣ a wanderer, a searcher
- ♣ combining the rational with the intuitive

As the primary champion in King Arthur's Court, the talents of this character come not from his powers of calculation nor his biceps measurements, but from a magical combination of forces, a special gift. Lancelot's fellow knights believed he would be the one to find the Holy Grail, but because of his love for the King's wife, Guinevere, he was not pure enough for a task of such high order, and his son, Galahad (the 9 of Clubs), achieved the Grail. Nevertheless, Lancelot stands out as a doer among the other cards within the rather dreamy Club suit. He is a Jack of outstanding importance and potentially one of the most powerful cards in the pack.

11 ♥
La Hire

A popular personality from fifteenth century France, La Hire's name (pronounced La Air) was used for the Jack of Hearts in the French pack for over three centuries. Numerous accounts of his bold escapades are still in existence, most of dubious factual content. The common thread between these stories, however, seems to be La Hire's unorthodox and fear-provoking battle tactics, as well as his untrustworthy nature.

Within readings, this card often portrays a young lover, the object of one's affection. This is natural enough, La Hire being the young male in the Heart suit. Despite the heartfelt affiliations, it is prudent to bear in mind the sly potential represented by this character. Remember the old nursery rhyme, "The Jack of Hearts, stole the tarts..."? Take note of the fact that this particular court is a "one-eyed" card. He is hiding something.

In the introduction titled "The Jacks," I mentioned that cards within this category are typically better behaved when "Mom" or "Dad" are around. In the case of La Hire, I believe it was actually Mom (the Queen of Hearts) from whom the tarts were stolen! Because this is

♥ a lover, a boyfriend

♥ sly, untrustworthy

♥ a hidden side, secretive

♥ unpredictable, rebellious

♥ a thief

the most unpredictable of the Jacks and the King and Queen of Hearts tend to be soft-handed, a good Spade or even Diamond ruler would be better "suited" to keep this knave in line.

THE ONE-EYED JACKS

In among the Lords and Ladies
That rule this curious pack,
There's a one-eyed pair of brothers
Both take the name of Jack.

At a glance they seem dissimilar,
Like night opposing day
Each looks his own direction,
Sees the world in his own way.

What's misleading, each lives separate
And serves a different Queen
But unless they're viewed together,
Leaves half a man unseen.

—CJF

11♠

Pampero

As fierce and predictable as the howling Pampero winds from which he gained his name, this Jack makes a loyal ally or formidable adversary. Traditionally, this card character is always pictured in profile. Unlike his one-sided brother in hearts, La Hire, who *hides* his other side, Pampero just seems to be *missing* any great dimension. These two are, in many ways, mirror opposites of each other. When seen together in a reading, the Jack of Hearts and the Jack of Spades create a synergy, one Jack complementing and completing the other.

Pampero's rather single-minded approach to life gives him the discipline and reliability not possessed by any other Jack. Like the steady wail of the Pampero winds, the Jack of Spades can oft be heard whinin' and complainin', moanin' and groanin' about this and that. No matter, it's usually just hot air.

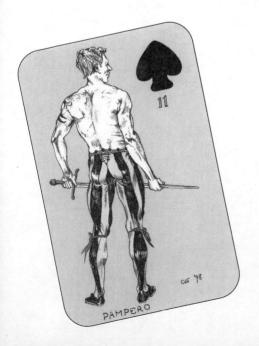

♠	reliable, loyal
♠	disciplined, predictable
♠	something missing, forgotten
♠	a whiner or complainer
♠	physically strong

THE QUEENS

TWELVE IS THE NUMBER ASSIGNED TO THE QUEENS, the four mature female personas of the playing deck. These are women with lifetimes of experience upon which to draw. Unlike the restless spirited Ladies, Queens are beyond the experimental personality phase. They have come into their own, so to speak, exuding the confidence of their respective suits.

Because each Queen's personality works in tandem with her mate (the King of like suit), your understanding of these cards will deepen as you develop your understanding of the Kings. You can think of the two personalities as limbs of a tree that grew and developed in response to each other. They fit. Marriages or partnerships can be indicated in a spread of cards by Queens and Kings of differing suits, although same or complementing suits allude to more harmonious pairings.

Queens commonly depict older women. They can also represent a younger woman playing out a more experienced, more mature part of herself, such as when taking on the responsibilities of a wife or mother.

12 ◆

Livia

This Queen is in many ways like the "first lady" of the deck. As wife to a very successful and public ruler, Livia has a dignity about her and knows how to play the supporting role. Though richly adorned by the wealth acquired from her high position within the Diamond suit, not all of this lady's values lie with her possessions.

When reading this card, I often imagine myself entering a room with a bright yet quietly burning hearth in its center. Livia's energy radiates a special warmth. Hospitable and kind, she represents many of the more positive aspects of the Fire Element. If you are looking for an honest opinion, you will get it from this Queen, though it will always be tempered by her positive outlook on life.

The bowl in Livia's hands is a very feminine symbol. It could be filled with anything. She is a receptor, a holder, a keeper of many things. It also corresponds to the womb and the ability to conceive children.

- ◆ honest, trustworthy
- ◆ wealthy, charitable
- ◆ one who plays a secondary or supporting role
- ◆ hospitable
- ◆ maternal
- ◆ receptive

12♣

Leah

As the female counterpart of the Club rulership, Leah expresses the intuitive, imaginative, and visionary aspects of our mental life, those associated with the right side of the brain. Because her domain is in a black suit, her powers are symbolic of night energy. Unlike the other Queen of Night, Morgana, whose earthy nature controls the denser kingdoms, Leah rules the lighter side of night: the dreaming, the mystery, and the knowing of the unconscious mind.

Mother of vision
Caretaker of dreams
Keeper of wisdom
Maker of moonbeams,
Sister to angels
Birds flutter in flight
Cradles your spirit
Voice echo at night.
—AC

To the extent that you can wish, believe, and envision, the power represented by the Queen of Clubs is awakened. The forces of magic wipe the sleep from their eyes, enlivening the spirit and opening the mind to possibilities never imagined before.

♣ a dreamer, a visionary

♣ imaginative

♣ intuitive

♣ delusional, given to fantasy

♣ an older or more mature woman of pronounced mental ability

12 ♥

Déja

Heart energy is perhaps most at home within the female presence. Déja possesses a softness that *is* her strength, a quiet knowing that dignifies her. The heart is an inarticulate organ, its mysteries lost to those who treasure words. The unconventional portrait of a court figure with closed eyes is a beautiful symbol of Déja's attunement to the inner world.

Unlike the other characters within this suit, the Queen embodies a rare intelligence of the heart, gained by years of experience. Hers are the desires of the wise soul, no longer distracted by more temporal attractions. And yet, Déja conveys a youthfulness not found in any other Queen. Herein the mystery of the Heart suit begins to unfold —the rebirth and renewal of Spring, the essence of eternity.

- ♥ emotionally mature
- ♥ sensitive, empathetic
- ♥ penetrating, focused
- ♥ withdrawn, reserved
- ♥ a wife of long standing, faithfulness

12♠

Morgana

Long abandoned by her nomadic King, Morgana is a Queen who has learned to stand alone. Popularly characterized in card games as the "old maid," the Queen of Spades appears strangely isolated, even when surrounded by friends and family. Life has made her tough. Morgana is incredibly strong and fiercely independent. But for all her strength, happiness largely eludes her. A secret sadness lingers beneath her exterior.

A legendary sorceress, Morgana is known for conspiring with the elemental forces of her realm in Earth. The cat in the illustration symbolizes this aspect of her character. Cats are often thought of as agents of magic and have long been associated with witchcraft. This is the darker side of the craft as compared to the more positive applications, which can be seen in the qualities of Leah, Queen of Clubs. Morgana's personality is frequently manifested as a need to control, manipulate, or dominate people or circumstances. In her determination to have her way, Morgana hatches her schemes, Queen of the hidden agenda.

- ♠ alone or lonely, isolated
- ♠ strong, independent
- ♠ discontent, unhappy
- ♠ secretive, manipulative
- ♠ a disciplinarian or one who dominates
- ♠ vanity, aging beauty
- ♠ the menopausal female

This image was inspired by a photographic self-portrait of artist Floria Sigismondi.

THE KINGS

CHARGED WITH SUPERSTITION, linked with the doings of witchcraft and the devil—thirteen is really just another number, isn't it? Take a closer look at the world that surrounds you, and behold! The number Thirteen repeats like a rhyme. Thirteen times the moon must travel around its mother, our Earth, to complete a year. Thirteen weeks must pass in order to complete each season, and round and round it goes. The number Thirteen has been described as the movement present in all things. It is a number of cosmic majesty, majestic, just as the Kings whose titles adorn these cards.[4]

The Kings are characters of nobility and stature. Their presence in a reading suggests authority, a governing influence. Each one's particular strengths are defined by the nature of the suit to which he belongs, his weaknesses by those to which he does not. For example, Sol, the King of Clubs, is grand ruler of the Air Kingdom. His strengths are born of that world. He is logical, educated, scholarly. In any of the other card kingdoms, Sol would be quickly overthrown. He does not possess any significant capabilities in the realms of Diamonds, Hearts, or Spades. In a reading, other cards can serve to fill in or make up for these missing aspects.

As you study each King, consider also the personality of the Queen who shares his throne, i.e., the Queen of the same suit. Like puzzle pieces, these two cards fit together, completing one another and creating a strong leadership. Typically, Kings will represent men of advanced age, experience, or responsibility.

---

[4] I have chosen to elaborate a bit here on the number Thirteen, unlike my treatment of other court card numbers. This was done in light of the significance this number holds within the playing deck.

13 ♦

King Leo

One important thing to realize about this King is his connection to the suit of Spades--an association often demonstrated by Diamond cards but probably symbolized most by Leo. Leo epitomizes strength of character and strong rulership on the Earth, the realm of Spades. Imagine Leo's Element, Fire, as it encounters the Earth, and you get the picture. This card represents a mover and a shaker, one who takes charge and changes the face of the way things are. His will is as a team of mighty horses, his temper as a raging inferno. Leo is also the big money card.

Other essential correspondences here stem from the fact that the Diamond King appears in profile, leaving one whole side of his person hidden from view. It is interesting that, historically, leaders often adopted this pose for portraits. It denoted power. Leo keeps a side unseen, a private world carefully hidden behind closed doors. As a King of great stature, this is at least partially done of necessity, as a retreat from the glare of public scrutiny. How true it is that we often see only what we want to see, usually just what we are shown.

♦ authoritative, powerful

♦ a man of finances

♦ courageous, ambitious

♦ arrogant

♦ temperamental

♦ one who keeps a secret life,
   a secret side

13♣
Sol

In long musty corridors lined ceiling to floor with volumes of science and philosophy, our Club King spends his days, absorbed in endless study. His skin has grown thin and white, transparent from lack of sunshine. His books surround him like a royal cocoon. The appearance of Sol within a reading indicates lots of book knowledge, years of schooling, a "heady" kind of person. Sol can be a lawyer, a scholar, a writer.

Whereas the Queen in this suit symbolizes the intuitive, imaginative aspects of Clubs, the King is much more logical, linear. Leah and Sol represent the right and left hemispheres of the brain, respectively. When united in a reading, they constitute the whole mind, indicating great mental capabilities. This can be going on within one individual or can manifest as two people who together form a synergy, something bigger than they are when separated.

Sol, perhaps more than other cards, is largely defined by what surrounds him. More Clubs would add to the weight of Sol's already highly developed intellect. Ideas are gaining precedence over life experience. Spades would indicate that the knowledge of this King is finding practical application. Diamonds and Hearts, as creative suits, would help Sol to think in innovative ways. Either of these last two also provide a balance of color, a red counterpart for a black King.

♣ knowledgeable, educated

♣ living "in your head"

♣ logical, linear, analytical

♣ a thinker rather than a doer

♣ a writer, information resource

13 ♥

Nichomiah

"Good King Nichomiah!" You can hear the crowds roar. King of merriment and sentimentality, Nichomiah rules his kingdom of Hearts, or does he? It is told his royal capes are so large only to accommodate the size of his overgrown heart. Whereas the Queen in this suit is *empa*thetic, the King is decidedly *sym*pathetic, generously dispensing of his wealth, even to the point of fault. Yes, in this world there are those who will take advantage of such a good-natured fellow.

While the music plays, the wine flows ever so freely and more plates of food are brought for the King's many guests. If not for the sober presence of his lovely wife, Déja, Nichomiah might lose the whole kingdom in a merry wager or give the royal treasure away to a clever-tongued scoundrel. This King wants only for others to be happy.

As a male card within a suit that is receptive by nature, Nicomiah tends to appear weak, especially as a leader. He exemplifies the shapelessness of his Element, conforming to what surrounds him. Comparatively, the Queen of this suit reminds me of Water as it becomes a wave: powerful, persistent and focused. Neither is good nor bad, but it is important to distinguish between different manifestations of the same energy.

♥ big-hearted, sympathetic

♥ generous

♥ sentimental

♥ conformable, compliant

♥ musical

♥ given to excesses of food, drink, etc.

13♠

Mardoc

As the last card within Spades, the suit of materiality and form, Mardoc assumes the role of terminator, the conqueror without mercy or compassion. His throne is the deathbed, the inevitable final stage of all Spade manifestations. This is a King whose castle has no walls, whose kingdom is limited only by the length and breadth of the Earth itself. His home is where he makes it, where his conquest demands. As such, this card will sometimes signify a loner or a wanderer.

Because of his position within the deck, Mardoc exemplifies a certain mastery and rulership over earthly affairs. Within a reading, the King of Spades will often symbolize a person of extreme efficiency and industriousness, a guy who brings home the bacon, or one who holds a position of authority over others, overseeing the practical end of things.

♠	a ruler over labor and practical matters
♠	stubborn, skeptical
♠	cold, unforgiving
♠	one who terminates
♠	a wanderer, one without a permanent home

Preparing For and Doing a Reading

In PART Two you will begin to slip into your card reading

skin as you move step-by-step through the process of a

reading. Preparatory techniques are covered first,

followed by card layouts and skills for interpretation.

Sample readings appear throughout.

But Before You Lay Out The Cards

WHEN DOING READINGS, it is important to recognize you are attempting something out of the ordinary. You are asking to see that which is unseen, searching for gifts afforded in higher dimensions, dimensions where future and past melt into the present. For this reason, many people find it useful to incorporate certain routines or rituals into their card reading practice. This can range from the very simple to the very elaborate. Rituals provide a transition, the all-important switch from ordinary life or our ordinary way of perceiving things into a state of heightened receptivity. This chapter is about finding that switch, learning to turn the knobs that bring new channels into view.

The ideas that follow are just that: ideas. Take what works for you, what fits your personal style. There is no right or wrong way to prepare for or do a reading. Never do you have to conform to some preconceived idea about what a reader says or does. Measure the value of your practices by the quality of your results.

I remember having my own preconceived notions in this regard blown apart as I called long distance to consult with a reader. After confirming who I was and why I had called, without any fluff or to-do about it, she just said, "So what do you want to know?" At the same time I could hear her crunching—eating something like potato chips. I was really taken off guard. This I had never experienced before. She made me rethink a few things about how a reading is conducted. Her sense of humor and non-pretentious manner throughout our conversation were very refreshing, and I got an excellent reading to boot.

The moral of this story is be yourself. The magic is in *you*. If a particular way of going about the reading helps turn on your receptivity, go for it. If not, why use it? You may even find some techniques work for a certain time and then lose their power. It is okay to experiment. Your own individuality will make your readings special and unique.

YOUR DECK

BE IT AN ORDINARY PLAYING DECK purchased at the corner drug store or one specifically designed for card reading (like *The Picture Book of Ana Cortez*), your deck becomes a tool of the sacred as you regard it that way. Accordingly, it is a good idea to keep a deck solely for the purpose of your readings. You may want to give it special treatment by keeping it in its own separate box or pouch. Cards, or any object for that matter, take on vibration and in time become a reflection of what surrounds them.

If you have a new deck or your old one has been busy hibernating in that special box you put it in, your cards are likely to be in need of some good old-fashioned energy, some battery juice. Spending time with your deck is the natural remedy for "cold" cards. It's like hooking up the charger cables. Your attention is electric and will give your cards power.

Don't fall into the trap of thinking that readings are the only way of doing this. My first teacher in card reading, Lainy, made an unforgettable impression on me in this respect. I remember her seated at the large table in my father's living room, alone with her cards for the longest periods of time. She would be talking and laying out different kinds of spreads, making up stories and forming alliances and relationships between the cards. I got the feeling I was watching a child play with her favorite toys. She knew her cards intimately. Each one was like a friend.

There is a word I like to think of when expressing the relationship between the reader and their cards. That word is *baraka*. It comes from old Arabic and is used to describe common objects as they take on uncommon characteristics. There is no equivalent for it in the English language. The wooden handle of an old shovel as it takes on the shape of your hand over time is baraka. A favorite pair of shoes as they form themselves to the unique shape of your own feet is baraka. Baraka means the object is so familiar that it becomes an extension of you.

Get to know your cards. Know their size, shape, and texture in your hands. Watch as they transform into baraka. In time, you can actually feel them taking on a life of their own. *They* will begin to teach *you.*

YOUR SPACE

THE SPACE YOU CHOOSE FOR YOUR READINGS IS IMPORTANT. It is special, just as your readings are. Once again, the only right or wrong is how it works for you.

Many people feel that a quiet, disturbance-free environment supports their readings best. Peaceful settings are conducive to concentration, give privacy, and fit with most people's conception of sacred space. Other less private settings, such as coffee shops, special events, etc., can work, too, as long as you are comfortable with it. I personally enjoy working in environments with a certain level of chaos as I find it brings energy to the reading and does not compromise the quality of what I am giving. Working in a public venue also rouses curiosity about what you are doing and can generate new business. Wherever you decide to conduct your readings, remember you will be asking sacred energies to come and visit. Tell yourself an honored guest is coming. Is your area clean and inviting?

Arranging your space can be a kind of prayer that adds to the total mood and consciousness of the reading. When the situation allows, I like to arrange an altar with each of the Four Elements present: a lit candle, burning incense (smoke makes Air visible), a dish of clean Water, and a small container of Earth. As Dianne Skafte relates in her book, *When Oracles Speak,*[5] an altar has the potential of being more than merely symbolic. She explains that the objects chosen "provide anchor-

---

[5] *When Oracles Speak: Understanding The Signs & Symbols All Around Us* by Dianne Skafte, Ph.D. Copyright 1997, 2002. Reprinted by permission of Quest Books / The Theosophical Publishing House, Wheaton Ill.

points in this world where the invisibles can dwell." In a fascinating and rare account, Skafte gives her readers a glimpse at a traditional Nepali Shaman as she prepares her ceremonial space. "Come, sit with me at this altar," the Shaman chants to the helping spirits. "Take your place on the thrones I have made in your honor."

PRAYER

IF YOU BELIEVE IN PRAYER AND USE IT IN YOUR EVERYDAY LIFE, this is a great thing to incorporate into your readings, too. You can say it out loud and share it with the person you are reading for or keep it private and say it silently to yourself. Prayer has the ability to put you in a state of consciousness that opens receptivity to subtle energies and your own intuition. It is a wonderful way to start a reading.

If you are not the type of person who prays but would like to try it, keep in mind a prayer does not have to feel religious or necessarily be what you think a prayer is supposed to be. If the word prayer bothers you, don't use it. You can substitute the word recitation or poem or blessing, whatever works for you. Above all, whatever you choose to do in this regard, it should be something you can personally relate to, something heartfelt. Say it with intention and meaning. Let your words have power.

An example of a prayer I have used is:

> *Father Fire, Mother Earth,*
> *Brother Wind, and Sister Sea,*
> *help us today to understand.*
> *Divine Spirit be with us now*
> *to guide this reading.*
> *May our hearts and minds*
> *be open to your messages*
> *and may our time together*
> *be for the highest good of all.*

The bare bones components of this invocation are: one—a call to whomever you are addressing your prayer, i.e., God, the Divine, friends in spirit, etc.; two—an affirmation of your desire to see the truth; and three—the condition that what you are doing be for the highest good of everyone. These three points can provide a useful construct for your own dialogues with the Divine.

With the prayer, you have in essence said "please" to your ethereal helpers, basically: "Please be with me now. Please guide me. Please hear me." It is just good etiquette, then, to acknowledge the assistance you receive by saying "thank you" at the end of your reading. This brings the session full circle and gives closure. Again, feel free to experiment with this and find what fits your own personal style.

My father is so funny sometimes; I love the way he ends a reading. Although he doesn't frequently do them, at the end, he is sure to give thanks. Silently in his own mind, as if addressing the figures of the court themselves, he simply says, "Ladies and Gentlemen, Lords and Ladies, thank you very much."

CONNECTING

THE WORD "CONNECTION" AS I AM USING IT HERE refers to the ability to tune in and really empathize with whoever you happen to be reading for. This is easier for some than others, but is something you can improve with practice.

Connecting is a phenomena that happens on an energetic level, a level more subtle and complete than simply a mental or thinking level. Having a strong connection with yourself, with your own presence, will naturally open you to being more sensitive to the energy of others.

You may find it helpful to set aside some special time before the reading begins to establish this link with the person for whom you are reading. If it suits your own personal style, take a moment and hold their hands. What do they feel like? Focus on your sense of touch and notice as much as you can. Connect. Become aware of the space between you and the person sitting across from you. Push your awareness to get bigger and bigger. Look into the person's eyes while tuning into your own breath. Relax.

What you are doing in essence is forging the relationship between your mind and body, expanding your perception to include all of your senses. This is the level where information comes in that surpasses ordinary thinking.

If you are conducting a telephone reading, you may have to adapt your technique. A simple method of connecting that works for me is to ask the person a couple of questions simply to get a voice imprint. Rather than focusing on the information they are giving, I open myself to just receiving and taking in the unique sound and quality of the voice coming across the telephone wire. I have also encountered readers who ask for your full name or full name at birth in addition to a birth date in order to "flip the switch" that opens the way for greater perception.

As your reading proceeds, check in with yourself. Have you maintained your level of connection? If you're not sure, you've probably lost it. Clues in this direction are a lack of eye contact, talking fast or for a long time without feedback, and fidgeting or other restless movement. The nice thing is you can always re-establish your connection. Take a deep breath and come back to the present. Pause or slow down your speech. Settle back into your bones.

Once again, we are talking about the mind/body relationship. Leaving your body is like walking away from someone who is trying to talk to you. Your body is an information receiving station. So often, the mind wants to steal the whole show. Be clear about what's coming from your connection and what's not.

This issue is a very personal one and needs to be approached in your own personal way. I find my own ability to "tune in" can fluctuate from one day to the next. It is a subtle and introspective science with many variables. Know yourself and you will know the world.

ASKING THE QUESTION

EVERYONE HAS A QUESTION, something that they wonder about or would appreciate some guidance on. More often than not, it is the reason people seek a reading in the first place. I always ask what the question is up front. A reading is no time to be shy. I am more interested in getting the issues out on the table, so to speak, so they can be addressed directly. This is vital because it focuses the reading, acting as a lens from which to view the cards. The very same spread can take on entirely different meanings according to the question asked.

One of the best ways to be of service is to help people phrase their concerns in a way that works in harmony with the nature of the cards. The playing deck, and oracles in general, function with profound, child-like simplicity and will reflect the inquiry in just such a manner. Complicated or ambiguously stated questions do not evoke the magic of the cards. Make sure the wording you choose is clear, simple, and direct, and the answer you receive will be the same. Beware of two-part questions disguised as a single inquiry. Break multi-faceted concerns down into components in order to get a clear response. If you're doing smaller readings, it's better to do separate layouts for each aspect of the question than to glob issues together.

When people want to know if they can ask a general question, I ask if they want a general answer. Like begets like with the cards. Similarly, it is interesting to notice where the person's inquiry is coming from. Is it from their gut or their head? A burning question is a world away from one asked out of mild curiosity. Surface questions get surface answers. Real questions invite the cards to speak.

One further consideration: when people phrase a question like "What is going to happen with _____?", remember that the future is not predetermined. It is an unfolding, the result of choices made now, in each consecutive moment. Because of this, "What will happen with _____?" can often be more helpful stated something like, "What do I need to know about _____ right now?" This provides the tools needed for the present. Present time is the only time in which change is possible, the only time in which we have choices. The "future," as revealed through the playing cards, or any other oracle or method of divination, is just a picture of what is presently being created. It is subject to change if and when we change. For this reason, a good reading is not always one that "comes true," but rather, one that brings awareness.

Finally, keep in mind that the deck is a one-year calendar, no more. Inquiries like, "Will I ever find the perfect job?" or "Will I live a long life?" are stretching into territories of time beyond the dictates of the playing cards and need to be reframed. "Will I ever find the perfect job?", for example, could be restated as, "What do I need to know about my job search?" or "What kind of job would be most satisfying to me?" or even, "What has been keeping me from finding a satisfying job?" The other example—"Will I live a long life?"—strikes me as kind of strange to begin with. This sounds like one of those surface questions we talked about, something asked because the person hasn't taken time to think about their real question. Of course, it is possible that they have a real health concern or have had a distressing premonition about their own safety. In this case, you, as the reader, need to uncover this and address the issue directly. Either way, I would encourage the person to take a moment and bring their real question to the table.

THE SHUFFLE

LOTS OF GOOD AND DIFFERENT TECHNIQUES FOR THE SHUFFLE EXIST, but a quiet, focused concentration is the common thread between them. This allows the cards to accurately reflect the topic in question. Mystical philosopher and physician Robert Fludd (born 1574) clearly states, "... *it is a general rule in this art that the soul must be in a peaceful condition and a condition in which the body is obedient to the soul; also that there must be no disturbance of body or soul, nor any bias concerning the question; that the soul must be like a just and impartial judge.... Likewise it is necessary for the practitioner to think intensely of the question that had been proposed so that he might not be seduced by any extraneous thoughts."* Although Fludd happened to be talking about the art of geomancy (of which he himself was an accomplished practitioner), his words can just as easily be applied to the playing cards or to playing cards in combination with geomancy, as will be covered in this book.

Thinking back to my late teens when I was first shown how to read with the playing deck, I remember being instructed to have the questioner spit into their hands before allowing them to shuffle the cards. A Lainy technique. This was supposed to put the person's energy into the deck. Needless to say, this didn't go over too well with many people and eventually I toned down the spitting part to having the person breathe into their hands instead. To this day I include the breath as part of the shuffle, partly in fond remembrance of my friend Lainy and partly because I enjoy a little drama in my readings. My point here is not to convince you to have people breathe or spit in their hands, but to re-emphasize that you can individualize as well as have fun with the way you conduct the handling of the cards. Always bear in mind, however, the one ingredient your shuffle cannot do without is concentration.

In order to give you some ideas for your own practice, I will relate the basic techniques I use myself. For smaller readings I ask the person to focus purely on the words of the question they are asking while handling the cards for whatever length of time they like. During this time, I also focus on the words of the question while simultaneously concentrating on my own breath and relaxing into my body. Some people shuffle for a long time, spreading the cards out all over the table or just mixing and separating them in different ways. Others give it the old one-two poker shuffle and they're done. My feeling about this is that each re-arranging of the cards is as unique as the individual and is perfect for them at that moment. I remember reading for a woman who didn't want to shuffle or rearrange the cards in any way. She just held the deck thoughtfully for a few moments, then set them down. She was following her own intuition and the cards, when laid out, reflected the answer to her question beautifully.

For larger layouts (such as the *Reading of Seasons*, p. 189), I recommend a more lengthy shuffle since a larger portion of the deck is to be laid out and a longer period of time is being represented. Because, in this instance, no single question is required before the cards are turned, I ask the person to shuffle while counting silently to themselves, backwards from fifty-two down to one. This is a powerful technique that thoroughly rearranges the cards and requires enough concentration to suspend the usual associations, putting to rest any mental "static" or energetic gobbledygook, so that, in the words of Robert Fludd, *"there be no disturbance of body or soul."*

Calendar Fun
and the 4-Card Spread

*T*HE 4-CARD SPREAD is the basic layout and has two variations, the Present Spread and the Cat Spread. Both are ideal for answering a single question and give a quick yet comprehensive reading. It is perfect for events or other public venues as well as for someone who has a "burning question" and just wants to "check in."

As your pack sits on the table, it is already in calendar form. The layouts are designed to simply expose little slices of time contained within it. Because the playing deck has 52 cards and the year has 52 weeks, each card naturally represents one week. In the 4-card spread, the top card of the deck corresponds to the present week and each card that follows is the passing of another seven days. The bottom card of the deck is 52 weeks from the present.

The real beauty and power of the 4-card spread becomes apparent as it is viewed in its relationship to geomancy (introduced on p. 141). Geomancy is a method of divination compatible to playing cards by virtue of its binary components. As you will see, the design of the 4-card spread is based on geomancy and facilitates a geomantic interpretation of the layout in addition to meanings derived from the cards themselves. Study this layout and its interpretation well, as it will be used later for the larger spread, The Reading of Seasons, in a more expanded form.

TURNING THE CARDS

HOLD ON. STOP RIGHT HERE. Before going on we must chat briefly about *how* the cards are turned. In the poem that follows, the playing deck is depicted as a book with the individual cards as its pages. As a practitioner (and budding expert in the *art* of card reading), always turn the cards as if you were turning a book page. Never flip head over tail, as is commonly done in card gaming. "Flipping" negates the nature of the deck as a book and reverses the original direction of the card, potentially altering the way the card is read.

The Two Sisters

Some say luck would claim a sister,
  An old spinster name of Fate,
  And both sisters scribbled volumes,
  Their adventures to relate.

Lady Luck composed her stories,
  Called Lady Luck's Romance,
  But she left them loose and scattered,
  So each page was turned by chance.

Well, her sister took these stories,
  Renamed them Fate's Romance,
  And bound them all together,
  So there's nothing left to chance.

In each case the story's written,
  And signed with fond regards,
  By both ladies claim to author,
  The Book of Playing Cards.

—CJF

The Present Spread

Yesterday's the past,
  Tomorrow's the future,
  But Today is a Gift,
  That's why it's called "The Present."

WHEN THE QUESTION ASKED INVOLVES A CONCERN immediately at hand or no more distant than one month from the date of the reading, the four cards for your layout come directly off the top of the deck. This is called the Present Spread.

After preparing the cards with the shuffle, turn the present card (top card) over first and the following three cards consecutively, placing each directly below the card previously turned.

Present card

2nd card from the top of the deck

3rd card from the top of the deck

4th card from the top of the deck

Taken together, these four cards provide a "snapshot" of the time at hand as well as the four weeks to come. Interpretation will be covered after we look at the other 4-card variation.

THE CAT SPREAD

THIS SPREAD GETS ITS NAME FROM THE AGE-OLD BELIEF in cats as beings who are sensitive to subtle energies. Have you ever seen a black cat appear from almost nowhere and scamper across the road in front of you? In times past, this would have been considered an omen, a message from worlds unseen. In the same way, this card spread singles out a moment in time, a time that is significant for the questioner. It reveals the cat's crossing place in our own lives.

After your deck has been prepared by the shuffle, ask the questioner to cut it once, forming two piles. Turn the card that is on top of the pile that was the bottom portion of the deck, the card that became exposed by the cut. This marks a spot within the 52-card calendar, the Cat's crossing place. Now mend the deck by returning the two piles to their former positions. The deck should be as it was before the cut, with one card turned somewhere within it.

Next, count four cards off the top and lay them face down in a stack. Repeat this, laying each new set of four down separately as you move across the table from right to left (see figure below). When you reach the turned card, stop. Commonly there will be one to three leftover cards between the last pile of four and the turned card. Just lay these face down in their own short stack. Now lay the turned card (the "Cat" card) face up on the table. At this point, your spread will look something like this, with less or more piles of four:

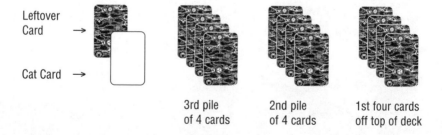

Leftover Card →

Cat Card →

3rd pile of 4 cards

2nd pile of 4 cards

1st four cards off top of deck

Because this is a 4-card spread, continue by turning over the three cards directly following the Cat card to complete your four card column (see the previous section, *The Present Spread*). Cards remaining in your hand are simply set aside.

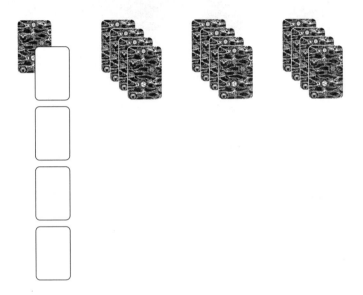

By arranging the cards in this way, you have actually formed a simple calendar leading up to the time specified by the questioner when they cut the deck. Each card is a week, right? Four cards makes four weeks, or approximately one month. Each card left over between your last pile of four and the Cat card adds one more week.

In the example pictured above, three months from the date of the reading is auspicious for the question asked (recall that each four-card reading begins with a question). Because each pile of four is slightly less than a calendar month (twenty-eight days as compared to twenty-eight, thirty, and thirty-one day cycles) and the extra week indicated by the leftover card adds a little more time, you have very close to three calendar months. Due to the irregularities in our currently used Gregorian calendar, adjustments must inevitably be made[6]. Let's look at one more example:

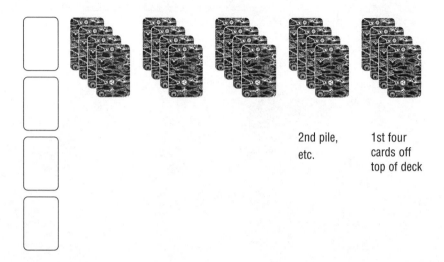

2nd pile,   1st four
etc.   cards off
                 top of deck

In this layout, approximately five months remain before the time specified by the Cat card. The cards came out evenly divided by four so there are no additional weeks to tack on. Again, because four weeks is twenty-eight days, the time indicated here is closer to four-and-a-half regular calendar months or five *lunar* months from the date of the reading.

If the question asked is directed at a specific known time in the future, the need for a random cut is eliminated. Say, for example, the inquiry is about an upcoming trip, i.e., the reading is taking place in the middle of April and the trip is scheduled for the first of June. The time in question is one and a half months or six weeks from the present. Turn your card clock ahead by taking the first six cards off the top of the deck

---

[6] For those of you interested in aligning your lives more closely with the cycles of the moon, you will be happy to know that the card calendar is a near-perfect representation of the lunar calendar. The deck comprises thirteen piles of four cards each, symbolic of the thirteen 27-29 day lunar cycles of the year. (From new moon to new moon averages twenty-nine-and-a-half days and is known as a synodic lunar month. A sidereal lunar month averages twenty-seven-and-a-half days and is the true period of the moon's revolution around the earth.)

(face down) and expose the following four cards. Abracadabra, you're looking at June.

When intuition directs, I will turn over the card on the very top of the deck because it represents the present moment and has importance for this reason. This card is separate from the 4-card column and does not figure into the geomancy. All other cards within the piles remain face down.

THE SIGNIFICANCE OF CARD POSITIONS

THE MEANINGS GIVEN TO EACH OF THE CARD POSITIONS within the 4-card spread are directly related to the meanings of the four card suits. Accordingly, as you develop your understanding of this layout, you will also develop a more intimate understanding of the suits themselves and the ways in which they interact with one another.

Once again, let us draw from the wisdom of the Elements as we consider suit placement in this spread. Fire, Air, Water, and Earth each have their own unique properties and functions. When determining which card position is governed by which suit, we look to the *density* of the Elements and the *body parts* with which they are energetically linked.

 FIRE: The Head

 AIR: The Throat

 WATER: The Torso

 EARTH: The Feet

Fire is the least dense of the Elements. It is expansive, ascending. As such, it takes its place at the top of the 4-card column. Its body part is the Head. Air is the next most rarified of the Elements. It rules the Throat and governs the card position directly beneath Fire. Water is heavier still and resonates at the level of the Torso. Earth is strictly bound to the laws of gravity and is represented by the Feet.

When looking at a 4-card spread, imagine you are looking at a person standing, a little person made out of cards. This gives you a working model of the person you are reading, allowing you to see which energies are operating at which level. It is a picture of the person in time, the time specified by the cut of the cards. Using only four cards, you will be able to give a detailed, multi-dimensional response to the question at hand. The following provides an outline for interpreting each of the positions.

◆ The Head Position

Ruling Suit: Diamonds

This card is sometimes referred to as the "Top Dog" because of its position at the top of the spread and its tendency to dominate the general character of the reading. It is the roof under which the other cards must stand. It indicates the consciousness or identity of the situation.

As it is governed by the Diamond suit, this card takes on additional significance in questions relating to finances, self-esteem, creativity (all Diamond issues), or questions specifically relating to the head, such as medical conditions of the brain, eyes, etc. It can indicate the appearance of the face and the reception of higher forces through the head.

The Throat Position

Ruling Suit: Clubs

The card in this spot relates directly to ideas and communications of all sorts. This includes legal documents such as leases, divorce papers, etc., and any other agreements, written or verbal, spoken or unspoken. It also signifies social relationships.

Rarely are questions directed primarily at this position, although communication relates to nearly *all* questions. People quite predictably inquire about money, career, love, health or housing issues, i.e., one of the other three positions. Because of this, the importance of the Throat card can be easily overlooked. The Club suit is subtle by nature, acting more as a *connector* than a center of attention.

One more note on this position: when teaching, I have been asked why ideas are associated with the Throat position and not with the Head. Good question. The Head position is related to mental awareness and overall attitude, whereas the Second position relates to consciousness as it becomes verbal, as it takes the form of thoughts and ideas that are ready to be communicated by the Throat.

The Torso Position

Ruling Suit: Hearts

Cards located in this third position are crucial to so many issues. The Torso includes the heart, the solar plexus, the womb, and the sexual organs. This makes it central in questions related to love, reproduction, and emotions in general. It also takes on significance in questions related to one's mother or questions that deal with hidden, unconscious issues.

Sex is represented by both this card position as well as the next position (ruled by Spades), depending on whether the experience feeds the heart or simply a physical need. Because

Hearts rule healing, also look to the card appearing in this position as an indicator of general health, vitality, and healing capacity.

More than anything, the Torso reveals the "heart" of the matter, the emotional environment surrounding the question, how one feels.

The Foot Position

Ruling Suit: Spades

This bottom portion of your layout corresponds to the most practical and fundamental areas of life. It is your foundation, the card upon which the others must rest. Even the best intentions can quickly crumble without good "footing." Look to this position for insight into Spade-related issues such as housing, possessions, career, daily routines, and living habits. Questions related to one's father can also be referred to the Foot.

Spade cards that might otherwise be viewed in a less than positive light can be dignified in this position. The Queen of Spades, for example, who has plenty of negative characteristics to choose from, could be a very desirable card in the Foot position, a placement that would emphasize her ability to "take care of business." Comparatively, the Throat position, for instance, would be a tough placement for Morgana, bringing out her poor communication skills and secretive tendencies.

Identifying relevant positions in relation to the question asked is key to using this layout. Before cards are even turned, you should have in your mind which card position relates to the question. This is the one to zone in on once the cards are laid out. Think in categories of questions. It's pretty easy since there are only four and they correspond perfectly to the card suits. A couple of brief examples will help to further illuminate the use of the four positions in your readings.

A young man once came to me asking whether he should consider a move. Since housing is governed by Spades, I knew that the Foot position card would be key in answering his question. He didn't have a time in mind for his move, so I allowed him to cut into the deck in order to find the Cat's crossing place (see *The Cat Spread*, p. 116). The time chosen was several months in the future and when the cards were turned, lo and behold, "The North Wind" (4 of Spades) was right in the Foot position. I told him there would be "a strong wind at his feet," but not until the time indicated by his cut. This kind of energy could move him quite a distance, certainly out of state. Note how this one card provided the answer to his question because of its position. The rest merely gave detail.

In another reading, a woman who confided that she had been trying to bear children without success asked if she would ever be able to conceive (Torso position). After reframing her question to "Will I conceive within the next year?" (remember the deck represents one year's time, no more), we laid the cards out to find the 6 of Spades ("The Ruin") in the third position. This did not paint a bright picture, and the geomancy confirmed her disappointment. Interestingly enough, the other three cards were all Hearts, showing her immense capacity for healing and love. I believe there is a great purpose in not being able to look beyond one year's time. It seems to me one of the highest rights of a human being is to be able to challenge one's own destiny.

Interpretation Techniques and Determining "The Weather"

BEYOND THE BASIC MEANINGS of the fifty-two cards, each layout contains a wealth of information for interpretation, if you know how to see it. Because cards, like people, behave differently in different surroundings, it is important to determine what those surroundings are. This is what this chapter is designed to help you do.

Patterns within the colors, suits, and numbers shade the reading, bringing out particular aspects of the cards. I like to think of this as the "weather" of a spread. "Bad weather," so to speak, or patterns within the layout that create imbalance or disharmony, will bring out those same characteristics in the cards, while "good weather" points to the more positive potentials.

SUIT PARTNERSHIPS

WITHIN ANY GIVEN SPREAD, identifying suit partnerships gives you a feeling for the overall flow of energies. As has been touched on briefly in the individual suit introductions (pp. 13-24), each has one other suit with which it is most compatible. These are the partnerships. Their presence within your layouts points to a flow and harmony, an alliance that supports success. Other suit combinations are less harmonious and present more of a challenge, no matter how positive the individual card meanings.

In thinking of suit partnerships, it is remarkably revealing to picture the suits as the Elements they represent and how they would behave together in nature. Fire and Air (the Diamond and Club suits, respectively) are natural playmates. Both are levitational (gravitating upwards) and thrive on each other's characteristics. Air feeds Fire, encouraging it to grow. Fire warms Air, exciting and animating it. Together these suits share the values of freedom, energy, ideas, and inspiration.

Water and Earth (the Heart and Spade suits, respectively) are both gravitational and find comfort with each other's tendencies. Earth provides a much needed vessel for the shapeless Water, lending security. Water nurtures an otherwise desolate Earth, making it hospitable for life. Together these suits share the values of security, dependability, practicality, and adherence to traditional values.

When partnerships appear in spreads, potentially negative card meanings tend to be lessened, balanced out, by the complementing suit. Note that each suit partnership represents a balanced color combination of black and red. When compatible suits are next to each other in a spread, a circuit of energy is indicated. These cards plug into each other, flow, complement, and empower each other. Black and red suits that are not partners (Spades with Diamonds or Clubs with Hearts) also create a balance of sorts but do not symbolize the compatibility and ease of flow that the partnerships do.

To illustrate, let's look at some simple card combinations that could be part of a larger spread. In a layout, let's say you find the King of Hearts (Nichomiah) next to the King of Spades (Mardoc). Here you have a suit partnership. Both of these Kings represent plenty of undesirable characteristics on their own, but because they are in partnership they can draw needed strengths from each other and create a balance. The side of Nichomiah that is overly soft and easily taken advantage of is fortified by the strong warrior-like qualities of Mardoc. Likewise, the potentially barbaric nature of Mardoc is softened by the big-hearted tenderness of Nichomiah. Together these cards create a better person, a whole. If, however, Mardoc were next to the King of Diamonds, or any other Diamond card for that matter, you would have a potentially dangerous combination. I would never knowingly give the King of Spades Fire to play with, unless he had a strong Heart card right next to him.

The Levitational Partnership	The Gravitational Partnership
————	————
freedom	security
energy	dependability
innovation	practicality
inspiration	traditional values

OTHER SUIT COMBINATIONS

THE RESULTS OF SUIT PAIRINGS that are not in partnership can be described as follows:

Diamonds with Hearts: A spontaneous and unpredictable combination, often indicating a lack of self-restraint and the tendency to act on emotional impulse. Feelings are expressed honestly and directly.

Diamonds with Spades: These two suits suggest a productive, self-motivated, entrepreneurial type of energy. People with this combination are strongly driven to make an impact in the world and have plenty of stamina to accomplish it; a real go-getter personality. There is a need to cultivate sensitivity and reflective thinking.

Clubs with Hearts: Air and Water are the two most sensitive of the Elements, giving rise to great subtleties of perception, emotionally, mentally, and intuitively. This makes for a fertile imagination and strong artistic/creative ability. A challenging, rather overly susceptible combination. Good for counseling and the healing arts.

Clubs with Spades: This is the opposite of the Diamond/Heart combination. It represents the ability to think things through in a very logical way and then apply that logic to the practical world. Mental, but only as it relates to "reality." Nothing unpredictable is going on here. Also implied is a tendency toward pessimism. Well suited for conventional business.

SUIT VOIDS

WITHIN A GIVEN SPREAD OF CARDS, it's not always simply what is on the table that determines the reading. How about checking for what's not on the table? In other words, what is the person *missing*?

Because the four suits represent such broad and vital areas of life, identifying which ones are absent often proves very tell-tale. No-show suits (or suit "voids") stand out like missing puzzle pieces. Solutions to questions are often found not in the cards shown, but in cards that are not. A good understanding of the nature of each suit is the foundation of being able to make use of this technique.

When only a few cards are turned, such as in the 4-card spread, a complete representation of the four suits is quite exceptional, indicating balance within the individual and a well-rounded approach to life. More commonly, however, one or more suits are missing. In these instances, voids become significant in relation to the question asked and, of course, your own intuition.

Consider this example. If in a 4-card spread you have one Club card, one Diamond card and two Heart cards, and the question is "When will I find a job?", then the absence of the Spade suit becomes a significant void, Spades being the ruling suit of occupation and labor. If the inquiry had been ruled by any of the other three suits, this void would not have taken on the same importance.

In the given instance, certain Spade qualities, like discipline and a regular routine, are apparently missing from the job search. Once consciously applied, the no-show Element is generated and the solution appears on its own. Because voids usually indicate an avoidance of the missing suit, in the given case there could well be a fear of being "tied down" by a job (as Earth, Spades are like anchors). This could be unconsciously preventing him/her from landing a position.

A positive geomantic show for this reading could help offset the lack of Spades and I would suspect that the job received would be somewhat unconventional, not involving a regular routine and probably related to healing, since the Heart suit was most abundant in the spread. Individual card meanings, their positions, and further geomantic interpretation would fill this reading out nicely.

In a large layout, such as the Reading of Seasons (p. 189), the question of balance between the suits can be viewed in a more general way, since you are looking at lots of cards and considering not just one question, but many aspects of the person's life. Picture a 16-card spread with lots of Spade cards, a number of Clubs, a few Diamonds and only one or two Heart cards. In readings like this, when one suit is so strongly represented, the compatible suit takes on a greater role. Remember, compatible suits balance each other, harmonize easily and temper aspects that could otherwise become negative or destructive .

By thinking in terms of the Elements these suits represent, the example given presents a dark, dry landscape with lots of Earth (Spades) and very little Water (Hearts, the compatible suit of Spades) to nurture it and give it life. The Spade suit is so chock full of negative card correspondences, this reading offers many grim potentials of manifestation. By giving more emphasis and attention to Heart suit characteristics, this person's life would transform.

Significant voids appear regularly and usually point directly to the cause of events that lead people to seek your advice in the first place. Is the person asking about the potentials of a new business venture and yet entirely lacking Diamonds? How about someone who is having trouble with their teenage child and has a weak show of Clubs, the suit of communication?

Checking for suit voids gives you an insightful way to view the overall spread and is a powerful yet simple card reading technique. Use it when appropriate, when your intuition tells you it is important. The following section, *Generating Suit Energies*, outlines ways to start bringing in the consciousness of individual suits to heal suit voids.

GENERATING SUIT ENERGIES

"It is through Earth we perceive Earth,
Water through Water, through Aether,
bright Aether, consuming Fire through Fire,
Love through Love, and Hate through grim Hate."
—Empedocles, *On Nature*

AS YOU WORK WITH YOUR CARDS, you are learning about the four suits in all their manifestations. You learn that they reflect the life of the Elements, the forces that weave the fabric of our being and attract the circumstances of our lives. You begin to understand that these energies can be consciously regulated to achieve desired results and bring balance and enlightenment into our lives.

A good card reading quickly reveals the current state of a person's inner Elements. In this way the cards become very diagnostic in the broadest sense of the word. You can think of the four suits as the four food groups of a healthy psychology. We need all four every day. Just as we can choose what foods to put into our mouths, we can choose what energies to align ourselves with, healing problem areas in our lives. By cultivating contact with any particular Element, we awaken and enliven it in ourselves, inviting it back into the circle of our experience. Below is a list of the four card suits and ways in which to generate their action within our lives.

♦ DIAMONDS: This is your internal Fire. Spend some time getting in touch with this Element. Watch the sunrise or sunset. Sit in the presence of burning candles. Build a roaring campfire and make an offering to it. Vigorous exercise generates internal friction and turns on your body's furnace. Give yourself an aerobic workout. Biking or a vigorous heart-pounding walk works wonders.

Seek inspiration through inspired writings or talks. Boost your financial confidence by keeping a $100 bill tucked into your wallet. It will make you feel wealthy every time you see it.

Prayer

*I give this day to the wisdom of Fire. Let your spirit
be kindled in me. Let me not stand outside your
circle of light, but let me enter into the life you give.
Burn quietly yet steadily in me, that I may go forth
with courage, confidence, inspiration, and strength.*

♣ CLUBS: This is your internal Air, the quiet and subtle Element in our lives. Stop and just notice the in and out flow of your own breath. Try doing this three times a day and see how your life is affected. Stretching and yoga are wonderful exercises that bring more oxygen into the cells of the body.

Connect with the people in your life. Strike up a conversation with someone you've never met before. Actively listen to what others are saying to you. Write a long chatty letter to a friend. Read a good book.

Prayer

*D*ivine *invisible breath. You connect me to magnitude.
Knowing you, I soar alongside the eagle and whisper
into the ears of all beings. Today let me listen. Let me
remember my quiet self, my ancient self, that I may
awaken to spirit, intuition, and insight.*

♥ HEARTS: This is your internal Water. Immerse yourself in this luxurious and healing Element. Ban quickie showers for a week and pamper yourself with long, decadent baths. Increase water-rich foods like fruits and vegetables and make sure you are flushing your system with enough fluids.

Look for and find opportunities to turn on the faucet of your feelings by expressing that which is in your heart. Give big warm hugs. Look someone in the eye and tell them how much you care about them. Write a love letter (to your lover, your future lover, yourself, your children, etc.). Start a journal of your feelings. Watch a sappy movie. Practice random acts of kindness and senseless acts of beauty.

Prayer

Precious Water! Your tenderness envelops me and washes me of my sorrows. With you I am comforted. Let me welcome your softness and fear not your depth. Hold me, each and every cell and fiber of my being, for you are my healing strength.

♠ SPADES: This suit is about your physical being and its relationship to our physical world. Get connected. How about a barefoot walk on our Mother Earth? Find a park with nice soft grass and have a no-shoes afternoon. Hug a tree. Start a garden or spend more time in the one you already have.

Nourish your body with good nutritious food and take care of it when it's feeling run down. Be nice to it. If you don't *give* your body enough attention, it will *get* your attention in increasingly unpleasant ways. Read the section on *Grounding*, p. 184.

Prayer

Dear Mother Earth, remind me of my roots — for I have forgotten. Fill me with your Earth vibration, that I may be strengthened. Whole. Without you, dear Mother, I have no physical form, no body with which to express myself, no wisdom with which to act on this Earth. Let all manifestations of you be kept holy. Let my actions today be my prayer to you.

NATURE SPIRITS
AS THEY PERTAIN TO THE ELEMENTS

AN UNDERSTANDING OF THE FOUR ELEMENTS can, as we have seen, contribute greatly to the interpretation of a spread of cards. When speaking the words Fire, Air, Water, and Earth, we speak of something that transcends mere physical or chemical properties. We speak of the life behind the Elements—the primary components of our human psychology as recognized by cultures throughout the world.

Stephen Arroyo, in his excellent book, *Astrology, Psychology and the Four Elements*,[7] refers to the writings of the medieval physician-astrologer Paracelsus in assigning a nature spirit to each Element, offering another potentially useful perspective for your readings. Although Arroyo speaks in terms of astrology, we can just as easily apply his writings to the Elements as represented in the cards. He states:

"These spirits, or their variations, are found throughout mythology worldwide and symbolize graphically how the Elements operate. This is not the place to dwell on the question of how "real" such spirits are, but a brief reference to the writings of Paracelsus here sheds light on how we can work with these forces. The undines were considered the spirits of Water, and Paracelsus stated that they must be controlled by firmness. Hence, we can learn that Water people need to be firm with themselves and also that firmness is often the best way to deal with this type of person, especially when their emotions are out of control. The spirits of the Air were said to be the sylphs, and they could be controlled through constancy. It is clear that a definite, consistent approach to life is something that the Air signs could well cultivate. Making a commitment with determined resolution is difficult for the Air signs, but it is an important step in their evolution. The spirits of the Fire are the salamanders, and they can be controlled chiefly through placidity. In other words, the Fire signs can curb the extreme uses of their energy by consciously cultivating a tranquil, placid state of contentment. If the Fire signs can learn this art of calmly accepting life in the here and now, they would avoid a great deal of stress and wasted energy.

[7] Arroyo, Stephen, M.A. *Astrology, Psychology, and The Four Elements: An Energy Approach to Astrology & Its Use in the Counseling Arts.* CRCS Publications, 1975.

The Earth spirits are the gnomes, which are to be controlled by cheerful generosity. Obviously, cheerful generosity is not a quality commonly found in the Earth signs, and it is therefore something they can all benefit from learning. And, I might add, the greatest strength and radiance of the Earth signs shines forth when they have assimilated this quality into their nature."

LOOKING FOR BLACK AND RED

WHEN INTERPRETING A SPREAD, it is useful to slightly unfocus your gaze and scan the cards for color patterns alone, putting aside pictures, individual suits, and numbers temporarily. In this way, you get a "color reading," providing basic insight into the layout.

COLOR CORRESPONDENCES

Black as Darkness/Red as Light   Black as Inner/Red as Outer

Black as Restraint/Red as Impulse   Black as Rest/Red as Activity

Black as Hidden/Red as Exposed

Ideally, you are looking for an equal combination of black and red that intermingle, demonstrating a healthy balance of energies. Spreads divided into distinct patches of separate color are characteristic of mood swings. This kind of pattern becomes increasingly evident in larger layouts.

As an example of how to incorporate color into your interpretations, I will relate a reading I once did for a woman requesting insight into her business venture. Out of the five cards turned (using the Cat Spread plus the Present Card), all were black except for one. Incidentally, the one red card was a low numbered card in Diamonds and most of the black cards were Clubs. The picture I got was "the Sun" (represented by the red card) trying to come out and shine on her endeavor but it was having a hard time because of all the "dark clouds" (all the Club cards). This person needed to turn up the sunlight by "putting herself out there" (red qualities) and let all her overburdened thoughts and inner concerns (black qualities) take a rest instead of call the shots. Simple color observation can enhance your readings a great deal and open your mind to metaphors that help you communicate in insightful ways.

MORE ON NUMBERS

AS DISCUSSED EARLIER IN THIS BOOK, the numbers pictured on the cards are one of the fundamental pieces of information provided by your deck. After you have acquired a basic understanding of what the individual numbers mean, you can start to identify and decipher meaningful patterns within your spreads. Included here are some of the more common and easy-to-identify ones.

Repeating Numbers: Like the individual rungs of a ladder, each number symbolizes a stage of experience to be passed through. Nature demands movement, and when several cards of the same number appear in a reading, it indicates stuck energy. The experience of that number has become a well-worn groove.

As has been touched upon, each number has a positive as well as a negative potential of manifestation. In expressing the negative or less enlightened aspect, we don't get the life lesson we are supposed to get and the experience is "dealt" to us again and again. This shows as a repeating number. Learning to view the positive side of a particular number releases it, bringing about a natural remedy for the situation.

Odd and Even Numbers: In general, odd numbers represent experiences of the inner life, introspection, challenge, and male energy. Even numbers signify focus on the outer world, solace from inner challenge, and female energy.

Low and High Numbers: A lot of low-numbered cards (six and under) imply lower levels of personal risk and weaker energy in general. High numbers (seven and above) represent high voltages of energy, bigger personal stakes and involvement.

CARD DIRECTION

AN ADDED POSSIBILITY FOR INTERPRETATION emerges as you become aware of the direction cards lie. I, myself, have never been one to "prepare" my deck before readings, i.e., making sure all cards face the same direction, although this can be done if you like. I know that people do this, especially when using Tarot, because when a Tarot card becomes turned from its original direction it is considered reversed and receives a different interpretation.

In my experience, there are no "reversed" meanings in the playing deck, as such. Interpretations can and do fluctuate, however, according to surrounding cards—what I have previously referred to as the "environment" of a spread.

The direction that any particular card faces holds significance in that it changes the physical relationship to cards around it. For instance, the direction a court card is laid will alter what that figure is looking at, reaching towards, or standing on, etc. Each spread is a collage of images showing how cards are interacting with each other. Lainy used to say that court figures standing upright were people "walking in" to your life and court figures upside down were "walking out." She got the idea of layouts as pictures. Let your mind make a momentary shift from mental analysis and just *look* at your spread. What do you see?

I remember once sitting and pondering over the meanings of a layout that had a number of cards with buildings on them, cards of the number Six. My daughter approached and, peeking over my shoulder, exclaimed, "Oh, look, it's a city!" I was shocked. She got it and I had totally missed it. It was her uncomplicated childlike manner of viewing the world that unlocked the mystery of the spread. Although this was not so much a matter of card direction, it illustrates the idea of simple, visual observation, which is what using the technique of card direction is all about.

Cards of the number Seven, the swords, are good ones to pay attention to in terms of direction. Which card is nearest the handle and where is the blade pointing? The power of Seven can be constructive or destructive depending on who or what is in control of it and where it is aimed. Is the sword pointing up, toward heaven, or down, toward earth?

Are there two or more swords in the layout, possibly indicating a battle of some kind? Asking yourself questions like this will provide you with glorious insights. In order to make use of this interpretive technique, always make sure you are turning your cards over from side to side, like book pages, rather than flipping them head to tail.

Something Old, Something New

Geomancy is old, very old, and so are the playing cards.

Together they create something new. This section of the text

unveils possibilities hitherto unknown in card reading. The

end of Part Three will expand your card-reading repertoire

with new layouts.

Divinatory Geomancy

*A*s mentioned, this system of card reading incorporates geomancy (pronounced gee-oh-man-see) to further define and enhance the information given by the cards. Webster's Dictionary defines geomancy as "a kind of divination by figures or lines, formed by dots or points, originally on the earth and afterward on paper." The word geomancy is derived from Greek and composed of *geo-*, meaning Earth, and *-mancy*, meaning divination. In naming it so, the ancients distinguished it from the other elemental practices of pyromancy (divination by Fire), aeromancy (divination by Air), and hydromancy (divination by Water). In consulting the geomantic oracle, we acknowledge our Mother Earth as a vessel of the sacred. We turn to our roots, humbly asking for "mother's advice."

You can certainly use your playing deck without geomancy, but why would you want to? Geomancy works naturally with the cards, is user-friendly, and will take your readings into new and exciting realms of possibility. You can even use geomancy without your cards. The truth is, both methods of divination stand complete on their own, but in combination, are a couple meant to be. Like a good marriage, playing cards and geomancy work hand in hand, surpassing what either could do alone.

Here I will briefly mention the existence of a different practice under the same name of geomancy, so it will not be confused with Earth divination as it relates to the playing cards. This other involves location studies and has recently become popular in Western culture via the Feng-Shui tradition. That is not the subject of this text. The practice

ILLUSTRATION 1: Medieval Arabic manuscript showing geomantic calculations for finding water. (MS Arabe 2697, fol. 16 Bibliothèque Nationale)

being explored here is a divinatory type of geomancy as opposed to a locational type. Questions of any kind are potential material for divinatory geomancy, just as when consulting the playing cards.

Divinatory geomancy is literally thousands of years old. Numerous theories exist as to its actual origin, but the most well established seem to point to the Muslim area of North Africa, somewhere around the ninth century A.D. (Stephen Skinner, *Divination by Geomancy*, Routledge & Kegan Paul, London. 1980, p.18). Then known as the "Science of the Sand," geomancy was a mystical art used for everything from finding water to determining the cause of illness. (See Illustration 1, p. 142.) The technique involved the tossing of stones or the random motions of a stick upon smoothed sand in order to determine geomantic "figures." In time, geomancy migrated north into part-Muslim Spain, where it gained wide attention. Paper and pencil replaced sticks and sand, and eventually geomancy grew to become one of the most noted sciences of the European Renaissance. During this period, geomancy came to be referred to as "terrestrial astrology," and was used in combination with the science of the stars to produce a prolific number of texts and charts for predicting the course of events.

So how do playing cards figure into all this? Playing cards and geomancy have made strikingly parallel tracks across history. Playing cards were in existence in Europe at the same time as geomancy and have also been traced to North African origins (see *Book Two*, p. 230). Over the course of time, specialty decks as well as playing decks have been printed with geomantic figures pictured on individual cards. This allowed the questioner to draw out a card and receive a ready-made geomantic response. (See Illustration 2, p. 144.) What does not appear in historical sources, however, is any reference to the fact that playing cards contain the components that *create* geomantic figures. (The re-discovery of the connection between playing cards and geomancy can be credited to my father, C.J. Freeman, and is discussed further on p. 220, *Book Two*.)

The deck is a book of unbound card "pages" inscribed with binary (or two-part) circuitry, the very stuff of which geomantic figures are made. The contrasting colors of black and red as well as the natural alternation between odd and even numbers suggest a mechanism, a machine for calculation. Binary mathematics has been in use for thousands of years in China and forms the basis of such marvels as modern computers. A small handful of authors, musing on the binary curiosities of the 52-card playing deck, have noted that the pack seems to have

ILLUSTRATION 2: Two cards from *The Astro-Mythological Game*, by Mlle. Lenormand, 1845, showing geomantic figures.

been designed as a calculator of sorts. But until now, no one has stepped forward to say what it calculates.

It calculates geomancy.

Laying out a spread of cards is like laying out a section of Earth upon which geomantic figures are cast. The four suits represent the Elements that weave the fabric of our world, the seasons of our environment, and the directions of the compass. Configurations of the suit symbols resemble spatterings of stones tossed upon the ground, as if in ancient geomantic ceremony. The integration of the two systems is like hand in glove. By their synergy, each throw of the cards blossoms into a multi-faceted act of creation, opening new portals of meaning, like doors to hidden treasure rooms, awaiting our discovery.

THE FIGURES

"*Geomancy is a Science and Art which
consisteth of points, pricks and lines,
made in steade of the foure Elements
and of the starres and planets of
Heaven, called the Science of the Earth,
because in times past it was made on it,
as we will hereafter declare.*"

—Christopher Cattan, Italy, 1558

DIVINATORY GEOMANCY IS BASED ON THE INTERPRETATION of sixteen
different "figures." The figures themselves are made of dots or stars and
look like clusters. Each cluster has its own name, divinatory meanings,
and governing celestial influence. These are listed below. The following
chapter, *Geomantic Calculation*, details the method of arriving at the figures using your playing cards.

Although the names listed here are in Latin, others exist in many
tongues. The given meanings are basically European. If you use your
imagination, the outlines of images can be seen in each one because
every geomantic figure is, in essence, a little dot to dot puzzle. New and
sometimes surprising interpretations can and will come up as you refer
to your own powers of observation and intuition.

* * * *	### VIA, ruled by the ### waxing phase of the moon ☽ The way. A life path, a street, or a journey. Singularity. An auspicious figure for travel.
* * * * * * * *	### POPULUS, ruled by the ### waning phase of the moon ☾ A crowd, a gathering, community. The tide of opinion. People as opposed to their rulers. This figure is reflective, mirroring its environment. Positive when surrounded by positive. Negative when surrounded by negative.

*   *
 *   *
   *
   *
	### FORTUNA MAJOR,
	### ruled by the Sun ☉
	
	Great fortune. Interior strength and protection. Safeguard. A good position in life. Success. A very fortunate figure.

* * * * * *	### FORTUNA MINOR, ### ruled by the Sun ☉ Lesser fortune. Exterior protection. Help from outside. Not very positive.

⁂ (figure)	**PUELLA, ruled by Venus** ♀ Girl. Daughter. Female employee. Pretty. Pleasant but lacking depth. Purity. More positive in questions relating to women.
(figure)	**PUER, ruled by Mars** ♂ Boy. Son. Male employee. Bachelor. Beardless. An erect phallus. A sword. Rash or inconsiderate behavior. The color yellow. Generally negative except in questions of combat or sex.
(figure)	**AMISSIO, ruled by the Venus** ♀ A loss. Diminishing. That which is taken or given away. Emptying out. Shedding an "old skin." Letting go.
(figure)	**ACQUISITIO, ruled by Jupiter** ♃ Acquisitions. Receiving. The increase of money or possessions. Comprehension. Absorption. Great benefit.

| ```
*   *
*   *
  *
*   *
``` | ### ALBUS, ruled by Mercury ☿<br><br>The color white. Pale or fair complexion. Dazzling. Brilliant. Wisdom. Clear thought. Positive for entering new ventures. |
| ```
*   *
  *
*   *
*   *
``` | ### RUBEUS, ruled by Mars ♂<br><br>A warning sign. Hidden issues coming to the surface. Passion. Vice. Fiery Temper. Accidents. The color red. Red hair. Ruddy complexion. Blood. Menstruation. |
| ```
  *
*   *
*   *
*   *
``` | ### LAETITIA, ruled by Jupiter ♃<br><br>Joy. Laughter. Expression of happiness. Health. Balance. Grace. Beauty. Bearded. |
| ```
*   *
*   *
*   *
  *
``` | ### TRISTITIA, ruled by Saturn ♄<br><br>Disappointment. Sadness. Melancholy. Blame. Sternness. Dwindling resources. The down side of things. |

* * * * * *	**CONJUNCTIO, ruled by Mercury** ☿ Connection. The lost being found. Relationship. Contracts. Agreements. Negative coming together with negative. Positive coming together with positive. Generally considered a neutral figure.
* * * * * *	**CARCER, ruled by Saturn** ♄ Confinement. Containment. Inaction. Delay. Prison.
* * * * *	**CAPUT DACONIS, or** **"The Head of the Dragon," ruled by** **the North Node of the Moon** ☊ Entrance. The threshold to the Upper Kingdom. Coming into. A positive figure.
* * * * *	**CAUDA DRACONIS, or** **"The Tail of the Dragon," ruled by** **the South Node of the Moon** ☋ Exit. Ending. Possible problems or complications. The Lower Kingdom. Good for terminating affairs of any kind.

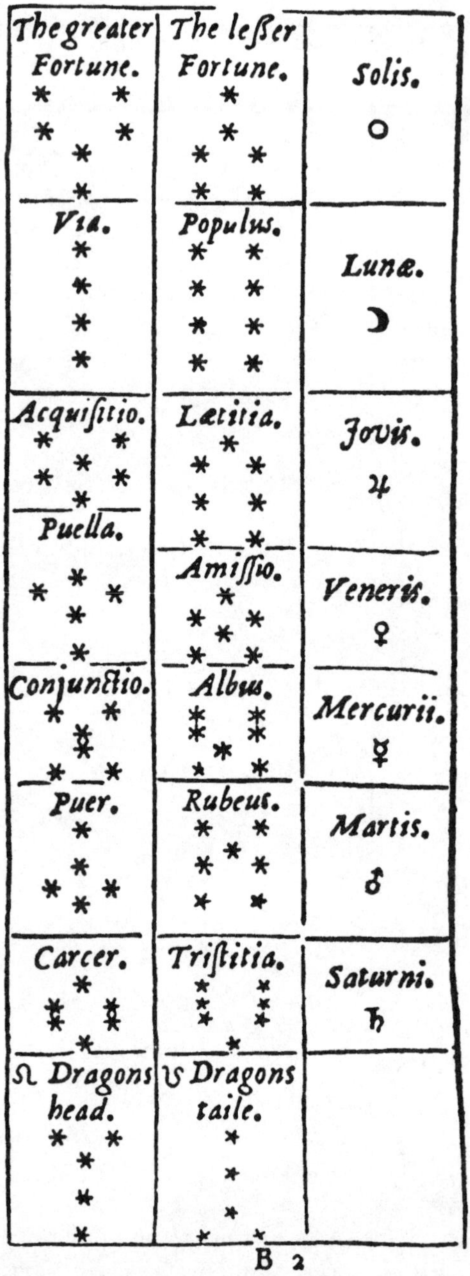

The greater Fortune.	The leſſer Fortune.	Solis. ☉
Via.	Populus.	Lunæ. ☽
Acquiſitio.	Lætitia.	Jovis. ♃
Puella.	Amiſſio.	Veneris. ♀
Conjunctio.	Albus.	Mercurii. ☿
Puer.	Rubeus.	Martis. ♂
Carcer.	Triſtitia.	Saturni. ♄
♌ Dragons head.	♎ Dragons taile.	

B 2

ILLUSTRATION 3. A table of geomantic figures from the *Fourth Book of Occult Philosophy* by Henry Cornelius Agrippa, London, 1655.

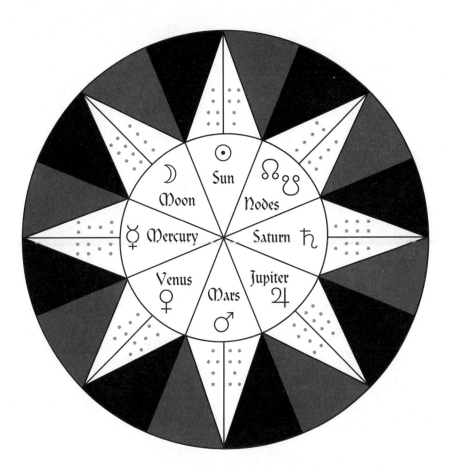

The Sixteen Geomantic Figures and Their Planetary Rulers

ILLUSTRATION 4. Geomancy written as viewed from the center of the chart. *Illustration by Ana Cortez.*

THE PLANETS

GEOMANCY MAKES USE OF THE SEVEN ORIGINAL PLANETS of astrology, plus the North and South Nodes of the moon, which are positions of the moon in the sky, not planets themselves. As already outlined, each geomantic figure has a planet or a node assigned to it. A basic understanding of these celestial energies will help to clarify your understanding of the geomantic figures ruled by them. The planets can then be used as a supplemental reference, further defining the forces at play in a reading.

The Sun: This is the primary source of energy for our solar system, the governing influence in our corner of the universe. It represents strength, leadership, and success. It rules health, authority, progress, and vital energy.

The Moon: This is obviously the closest planet to home and affects life on this Earth very deeply. Its energy is of the female, the Mother. It governs moods, feelings, instincts, the unconscious, and habit patterns. Its vibration is receptive and reflective, mirroring surrounding influences.

Mercury: This planet is personified in mythology as the silvery-winged messenger. Its action is quick and electric. Mercury rules mental processes, written and oral communication, and the ability to connect and relate things together. Because it is the messenger, Mercury can also symbolize travel and transportation.

Venus: Often thought of as "the planet of love," Venus covers the full spectrum of affections including tenderness and vulnerability, sentimentality, art and aesthetic appreciation, pleasures and pleasantries. Venus represents sensuality as opposed to sex.

Mars: The symbol for Mars is of a shield and spear. The mode of operation is sudden and assertive. Mars governs ambition, competition, weapons, war, accidents, and violence. It also represents sex and our primal animal nature. Mars' energy can be used destructively and angrily or can give courage and strength.

 Jupiter: This is the largest planet of our solar system, actually exceeding the mass of all the other planets combined. Jupiter reflects this energetically, representing expansion and growth. It indicates receiving, prosperity, optimism, expressions of joy, and good luck.

 Saturn: This is the taskmaster of our celestial sphere. It involves life lessons and working through karma. Saturn governs delays and disappointments, discipline and patience, aging and wisdom. Its vibration is slow, serious, and deep.

North

South

The Nodes: These are the two places in the sky where the path of the Moon meets the path of the Sun, where their footprints cross as viewed from the Earth. It is where eclipses occur. Taken together, these two Nodes form an axis. The North Node represents beginnings, openings, and directions to strive for. The South Node corresponds to endings, lessons already learned and areas of our lives that do not offer growth.

Geomantic Calculation

*A*S HAS BEEN MENTIONED, geomantic calculations work very naturally with the playing deck. The additional correspondences give an added dimension to readings that allows for greater accuracy and interest. The calculation of geomantic figures is actually quite simple, despite the deceptively long explanations that follow. With a little practice, it can be done within a few seconds after the cards are laid out.

The spreads in this book were specifically designed to facilitate the rendering of the sixteen figures of geomancy. Both the 4-card layout and the Reading of Seasons consist of columns, which is exactly what geomantic figures are. Let's take a closer look:

FORTUNA MAJOR
       *   *
       *   *
         *
         *

Here, we see a cluster of stars making the configuration known as "Fortuna Major." This figure, like all geomantic figures, is made up of four separate tiers or levels, just like your card spreads.

FORTUNA MAJOR

1.   *   *

2.   *   *

3.   *

4.   *

With this diagram, we can see how the figure is constructed. Each level consists of either one or two markings. In the case of Fortuna Major, from top level to bottom level you have two, two, one, one. For the sake of our calculations, we'll refer to a single mark as odd and a double mark as even. Let's take another example:

PUELLA

Looking at this figure by levels you have (from top to bottom): odd, even, odd, odd. Simple, yes? All geomantic figures are constructed similarly, and when every possibility is drawn out, you get a total of sixteen combinations or sixteen figures.

One of the fun things about geomancy is that anything you can count can be used to determine your figure. All numbers are odd or even, right? Any number can be given a shorthand notation of a single or double star.

Historical tidbit: Since geomancy literally means 'Earth divination,' one practice in times past was to use roots as geomantic oracles. After being planted and harvested according to particular instruction, potatoes would be chosen and the number of eyes would indicate an odd or even marking. Four potatoes would render all four sections of a figure and an answer could be given to the question asked. But enough about potatoes for now; let's return to cards.

Playing cards, of course, all have a number assignment. The Aces are one, the Twos are two, etc. Court cards simply fall into sequence after the Nines. Lady cards have a value of ten, Jacks are eleven, Queens are twelve, and Kings are thirteen. *The Picture Book of Ana Cortez* has the number value of all the courts written on the cards themselves. This will assist you with your geomantic calculations.

Now let's imagine a 4-card spread consisting of (from top to bottom): the 6 of Spades, the 7 of Spades, the King of Hearts, and the 8 of Diamonds. Voila. Your layout produces a geomantic figure:

Let's try another one. This time your cards will be: the 2 of Hearts, the 3 of Spades, the 10 of Clubs, and the Ace of Diamonds.

All this would end right here if it were not for the fact that playing cards have not one but *two* binary devices built into them: numbers *and* colors. The traditional colors of black and red also point to a binary or two-part possibility of calculation.

Now the question arises: which color will be odd and which will be even? To use the colors in a binary way, this must somehow be assigned, and yet the colors themselves do not allude to an odd or even affiliation and the deck gives no further clues in this direction. Certainly there are both odd and even numbered cards within each black and red suit. Is it possible that the colors could be odd *or* even? That red, for instance, could indicate an odd marking in some spreads and an even marking in others? Could the particularities of each individual spread dictate the association?

One way to look at your layouts is to think of them as recipes. Each card is like a different ingredient that combines with the others to create a new and different "dish" every time a spread is laid out. Since the meanings of individual cards alter as they interact and blend with one another, a changing affiliation for the binary meaning of the colors would reflect this shape-shifting feature of the deck. Since numbers must be permanently odd or even, it seems necessary and important that the colors be free to change.

So how does all this come together in practice? After arriving at a geomantic figure according to number, some simple addition is needed to determine your geomancy by color. Here is one of the examples we looked at earlier:

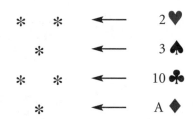

Acquisitio
(geomancy by number)

The first order of business is to determine which color will be odd and which will be even for this particular spread. Help is on the way when we recall that each position in the layout has its own special meaning (see *The Significance of Card Positions*, p. 119). The top card is in the Head Position and is key in determining the general character of the reading. As such, it is perfect for use as a color indicator. In the given example, the Head Position card happens to be the 2 of Hearts: a red card. We will now find the *total value* of red for this layout by adding the value of all cards that share this color. Looking at our spread then, we see one more red card in addition to the 2 of Hearts: an Ace. Adding the value of these together, we get three, since two plus the Ace equals three. This gives our key color an odd value and red becomes odd for this reading. Black becomes even, simply by default, and we can calculate our geomancy by color.

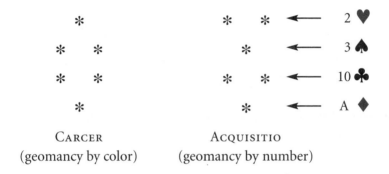

CARCER   ACQUISITIO
(geomancy by color)   (geomancy by number)

You now have two geomantic figures to complement your reading. Notice how the figures are written from right to left, the opposite direction of our Western style of writing. For the length of its history geomancy has been figured this way, a remnant of its Arabic origins. Soon you will discover the significance of keeping your geomancy by number on the right and your geomancy by color on the left, but for now, let's do a little more homework. Here is your next layout:

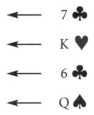

Always figuring the geomancy by number first, make sure to write your findings on the far right side of your paper. Here you have a Seven, which is odd; a King, which is also odd; a Six, which is even; and a Queen, which is even.

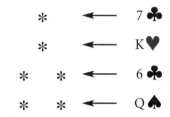

FORTUNA MINOR
(geomancy by number)

Now to find the geomancy by color, look to the top card, which in the given instance is black. Determine the total value of black for this spread by adding the numbers of all black cards. Seven plus six plus Twelve (the value of a Queen) gives us a grand total of twenty-five, an odd number. For this layout then, black is odd and red automatically becomes even. Your math sheet now becomes:

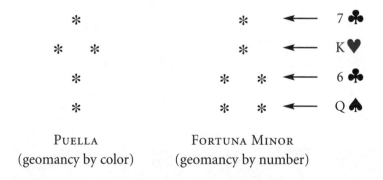

PUELLA   FORTUNA MINOR
(geomancy by color)   (geomancy by number)

An alternate method of doing your math that is substantially less time consuming and less prone to error is to reduce the numbers to odd or even *before* adding them. This is called binary addition. In the previous example, instead of adding seven plus six plus twelve, simply add together odd plus even plus even. Pictorially you get: ∗ plus ∗∗ plus ∗∗, which equals ∗∗∗∗∗. The answer is five, or odd, just as the answer was odd when adding the full value of the numbers.

After a small amount of practice you'll be impressing yourself with how quickly you can figure your geomancy by color. Binary addition is the secret, just as it is the secret to the amazing speed of modern day computers. Now try this one:

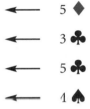

The first figure (geomancy by number) should be obvious. If you had trouble, backstroke a bit and review the foregoing examples.

CAUDA DRACONIS
(geomancy by number)

To find the second figure, we look to the top card, which happens to be red. Because in this instance there are no other cards of this color in the layout, we can skip the addition and just use the value of the top card alone as the color indicator.

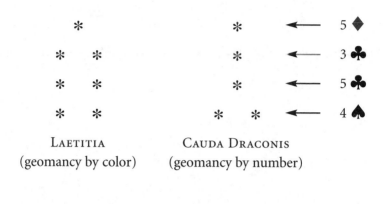

LAETITIA
(geomancy by color)

CAUDA DRACONIS
(geomancy by number)

Practice makes perfect, so here are some sample 4-card spreads to polish your skills. The answers follow.

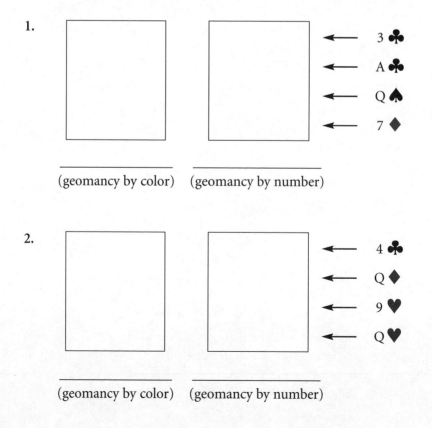

1.

(geomancy by color)   (geomancy by number)

2.

(geomancy by color)   (geomancy by number)

3.

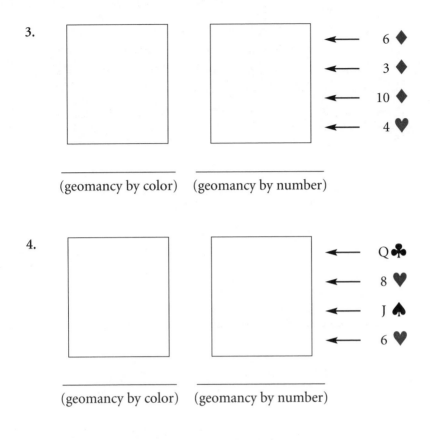

← 6 ♦

← 3 ♦

← 10 ♦

← 4 ♥

_____   _____
(geomancy by color)   (geomancy by number)

4.

← Q ♣

← 8 ♥

← J ♠

← 6 ♥

_____   _____
(geomancy by color)   (geomancy by number)

~

ANSWERS: 1. geomancy by number is Puer, by color is Tristitia.

2. geomancy by number is Albus, by color is Caput Draconis.

3. geomancy by number is Rubeus, by color is Via.

4. geomancy by number is Albus, by color is Amissio.

~

Using the last spread from the above worksheet, we will follow the reading through to see how the two separate figures work in tandem to supplement the reading. Here is the layout and the figures it yields:

✳	✳ ✳	⟵ Q ♣
✳ ✳	✳ ✳	⟵ 8 ♥
✳	✳	⟵ J ♠
✳ ✳	✳ ✳	⟵ 6 ♥

AMISSIO	ALBUS
(geomancy by color)	(geomancy by number)

These two initial figures formed by number and color are known in geomantic terms as Witnesses. Together they work hand in hand to reveal different aspects of the question asked. Two separate methods exist for interpreting the Witnesses, either of which work very nicely during a reading.

The first and probably most common way to use the figures is to create a simple time line. The first Witness (geomancy by number) indicates the beginning stages of the situation in question, and the second Witness (geomancy by color) corresponds to the unfolding of circumstances as time progresses. I like this method because it allows the reader to see a development of events.

So, looking at the above layout, let's say the question asked was, "Should I go back to school in the fall?" The first Witness, Albus, is a figure representing clear thinking and is also a positive figure for beginnings. This is obviously a good sign and especially auspicious for a question related to schooling and the acquisition of knowledge, since Albus is ruled by Mercury, and other meanings include wisdom, brilliance, etc. (see *The Figures*, p. 145).

The second Witness, Amissio, characteristically points to a loss of some sort. In the given instance, I suspect it would be related to finances since there is a complete absence of Diamonds in the spread, the suit associated with money. There could also be issues related to motivation or self-esteem, as these are other attributes of the Diamond suit. This, by the way, is a beautiful example of a suit void that has become significant by way of the geomancy. So, summing up what we have seen so far, after a positive beginning and good intentions, eventually the suit of Diamonds will need to be addressed in order for this person to continue what they started.

Notice how all this insight has come primarily from geomantic observation, without yet considering individual card meanings. The geomancy gives your reading a particular "slant," taking it in certain directions and helping you to then interpret the remaining correspondences in the spread. The card meanings and the geomancy work in conjunction to create a strong and detailed reading.

The other method of interpreting the Witnesses is to view them as two separate aspects of the individual. The first Witness, being derived by number, corresponds to the rational, logical side of the self. Interestingly, this is the Witness on the right hand side of the paper, connecting it to the left side of the brain. This part of our being deals with numbers and our linear, logical ways of perceiving the world. The second Witness, the figure derived by color, corresponds to our emotionally driven responses and the right side of the brain. This is what people feel in their gut but can be unaware of intellectually.

Using this second method to interpret the same reading, the figure of Albus symbolizes this person's rational self, their cognized intention of going to school. The Queen of Clubs in the prominent top position of the layout further confirms this insight. Leah is a character whose dreams are clearly envisioned.

Now we turn to Amissio. Here we find reflected a feeling of loss on some level, a feeling quite separate from the optimism of his/her intellect. Again, because of the absence of Diamonds, I suspect that this may be connected with finances or possibly self-confidence. The person is aware of this emotionally but has not fully grasped it intellectually. Recall also that Diamonds is the companion suit for Clubs. Diamonds embody the fiery dynamic that would illuminate and energize our school-going Air Queen, Leah. But before drawing any final conclusions, we will now proceed to the very last geomantic calculation for the four cards: the Judge. As in any good court of law, the Witnesses must appeal to the Judge in order to receive a verdict. According to geomantic tradition, two figures must yield a third.

Continuing with the same sample reading, we will combine the initial figures of Albus and Amissio by using the binary addition we already know to get a third and totally new figure. Moving as always from right to left, our final calculations become:

Odd	*	=	*	← plus	*	*
Even	* *	=	* *	← plus	*	*
Even	* *	=	*	← plus	*	
Even	* *	=	* *	← plus	*	*
	LAETITIA		AMISSIO		ALBUS	
	(Judge)		(2nd Witness)		(1st Witness)	

So the general answer to the question, in this case, is represented by Laetitia. Relating this to our example, despite the loss suggested by Amissio, the final outcome appears positive, as meanings for Laetitia include outward expressions of joy, laughter, etc. Referring back to the actual cards that were used to determine these figures, we can see that the meanings here are also quite positive, further supporting an affirmative answer. Details could be clarified according to additional information contained in the spread and through the intuitive connection between the reader and the inquirer. Always remember that the geomancy and the card correspondences work together to form a total picture.

The following provides a table of reference for interpreting the three figures in your readings. As always, I invite you to question authority and consult with your own *inner* table of reference (called intuition) as well.

1. Two good Witnesses resulting in a good Judge is very fortunate.

2. Two unfortunate Witnesses resulting in an unfortunate Judge is naturally unfortunate.

3. If the two good Witnesses produce an unfortunate Judge, conditions favor the attainment of the goal, but success will be bittersweet.

4. If two unfortunate Witnesses produce a good Judge, continuing hardships finally end in good fortune, but probably not the fortune expected.

5. If the first Witness is bad and the second good, difficult beginnings take an unexpected turn for the better. Results will be indicated by the Judge.

6. If the first Witness is good and the second bad, success will be more difficult to obtain, regardless of the Judge.

Further Geomantic Indications

Aside from the standard meanings of each geomantic figure, further insight can be gained by observing how the special features of each figure relate to specific cards within the spread. For example, let's look at Caput Draconis or "The Head of the Dragon," a figure indicating an entrance, a new beginning or threshold.

```
*    *    ◄——— Head

   *      ◄——— Throat

   *      ◄——— Torso

   *      ◄——— Foot
```

Here we see that the top line, the Head, is obviously different than the bottom three lines. It stands out visually. Following this observation, we know that when "The Head of the Dragon" appears in a reading, the card in the top position of the spread is likely to gain significance. To further illustrate, let's take a 4-card reading I once gave to a woman inquiring whether or not home schooling was a good option for educating her children. The cards laid out and the resulting figures were as follows:

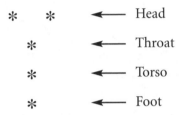

```
*    *    =    *    *        *    *    Q♥    ◄——  Head

*    *    =    *             *         7♠    ◄——  Throat

*    *    =    *             *         7♣    ◄——  Torso

   *      =    *         *    *        10♣   ◄——  Foot
```

Tristitia	Caput	Conjunctio
(Judge)	Draconis	(1st Witness)
	(2nd Witness)	

Among other very interesting dynamics indicated in this reading, the Queen of Hearts is significant in relation to the second figure, Caput Draconis, by its position in the spread. Apparently, the qualities of love and devotion represented by this card are standing at the threshold of home schooling. This impulse of love is leading her into a search for a new kind of education for her children. The first geomantic figure of Conjunctio symbolizes a coming together, well pictured by the two lines of even markings in the Head and Foot positions, connected by the singular dots in the middle positions. Looking at the cards in the Head and Foot positions, we see that women are coming together, feminine energies, and this is also important to this woman.

Finally, the judge, Tristitia, points to the Foot position card as especially relevant to the disappointment associated with this figure. Here, we find Fortuna, carefree as a Sunday breeze. After the hopeful start represented by Caput Draconis and Conjunctio, the inconsistent nature of Fortuna forebodes a poor result. Indeed, the Foot position, being the natural home of Spades, the suit of discipline and hard work, is hardly dignified by the whimsical nature of the 10 of Clubs, especially for such an ambitious undertaking as home schooling. This client needed to take a serious look at her own ability to commit to the labors needed for such a venture. As you can see, this kind of geomantic observation is extremely useful.

CONNECTING THE DOTS

GEOMANCY IS A VISUALLY STRIKING METHOD OF DIVINATION. This is part of its magic and its power. Explore this feature of geomancy by using geomantic dots as templates for new creations. It's fun to just sit and doodle with geomantic figures. Often I find that this brings out meanings I otherwise would not have been aware of. When a particular figure carries importance in a reading, I like to give a decorative drawing of it to the questioner. This then becomes a personal symbol for them and also helps to make the reading more memorable. Here are some sample doodlings to spark your own artistic intuition:

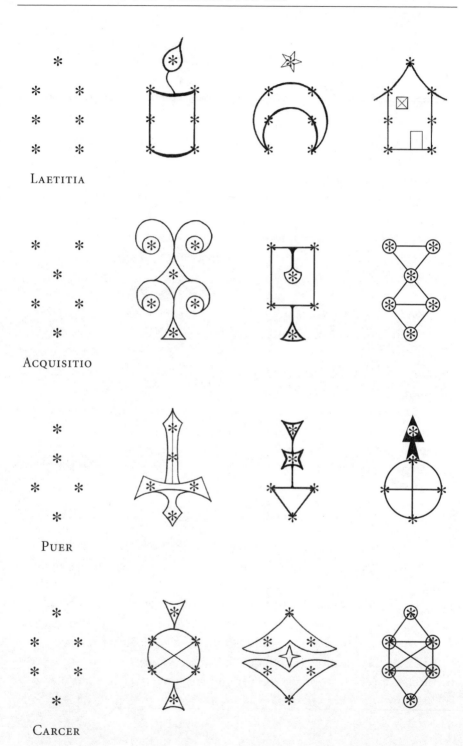

LAETITIA

ACQUISITIO

PUER

CARCER

*A*lternate *S*preads and *L*oose *E*nds

THE LOST MAN SPREAD

THIS SPREAD IS A GOOD ONE TO USE when you want to get a feel for surrounding influences, for the ambient environment of a particular person or concern. The whole technique is refreshingly uncomplicated.
Forget about the calendar and geomancy for this one. After deciding
who or what your question is about, simply assign it a card in your own
mind, shuffle, shuffle, shuffle, then spread the deck out and find it. Once
you have found your "lost" card, look to see where it put itself, that is to
say, observe which cards it likes for company. With the Lost Man, you
get a candid camera picture of your concern in its natural habitat. Cards
closest to the card assigned represent the strongest influences. Cards
further away have a correspondingly weaker influence.

Now let's consider some sample questions and the cards that could
be assigned to represent those questions in a spread. First, imagine that
someone has come to you with a health concern. Hmmm . . . What do
you think would be a good card to symbolize this? How about using the
7 of Hearts, the "Sword of Healing"? Another example. What if someone
living in the Midwest is worried about an upcoming trip to the East
Coast? One possible choice would be the 4 of Clubs, "The East Wind."
This would represent the direction of travel. Are you getting the idea?

Now we come to the matter of assigning a card when the inquiry is
about a person. Well, we do have sixteen court cards to choose from,
but which one? One method is to simply decide which court card is
most similar to the person in question based on personality traits. A
middle-aged man who works in the psychology department of a
university, for example, would be a good match for the King of Clubs,

an older male court card representing the attainment of knowledge and educational status.

Another method, which I actually prefer, is to assign a card based on the Element of the birth date. Because each sign of the zodiac is associated with either Fire, Air, Water, or Earth, each of us has a suit we are born into. You could say this is your Birthday Suit! The twelve signs and the Elements they correspond to are listed below. A basic astrology book will give you the cut-off dates for each.

FIRE	EARTH	AIR	WATER
Aries	Taurus	Gemini	Cancer
Leo	Virgo	Libra	Scorpio
Sagittarius	Capricorn	Aquarius	Pisces

Using the chart above to determine the suit (and keeping in mind the person's gender and age category), an older man born in mid-February (Aquarius) would be represented by the King of Clubs, Clubs being the suit associated with Air. The point here is to disregard the personality altogether and refer instead to the birth date. This actually gives this method its strength. It allows you to know less detail about the person, reducing the possibility of coloring the reading with opinions formed beforehand.

I have found that those who already possess a working knowledge of astrology are most comfortable with this method. If figuring the birth date adds confusion to your readings, let it go. The important thing is to assign a card that makes sense to you and to fix that card in your mind. Your intention sets the magic into motion.

Now let's sit in on an actual Lost Man reading. A woman who once came to me (we'll call her Mrs. H) was worried about her son (we'll call him M). Apparently, M had recently gone off to college and was getting into trouble with some fellow fraternity brothers. Mrs. H gave me his birth date, which happened to be in Scorpio, a Water sign. In my own mind then, I assigned the young male court card in the Water Element, the Jack of Hearts, to represent M (remember, none of the personality traits normally associated with La Hire come into play here, as we are using only the birth date in assigning this card). After Mrs. H shuffled, the deck was spread across the table, face up. The "lost" card was then located among the following:

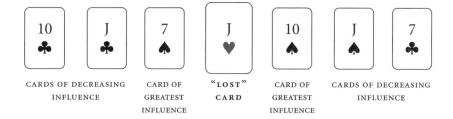

CARDS OF DECREASING   CARD OF   "LOST"   CARD OF   CARDS OF DECREASING
INFLUENCE   GREATEST   CARD   GREATEST   INFLUENCE
                  INFLUENCE   INFLUENCE

Focusing first on the colors and suits, I said to Mrs. H, "Your son is a good friend to many. He gives a lot and enriches the lives of those around him." This is witnessed by the fact that the Jack of Hearts is the only Water card in the vicinity, actually the only red card at all. It also happens to be surrounded on both sides by Earth, the Element that depends on Water for life and sustenance.

Observing further, "I also see a relationship between your son and a very special female who gives him much strength and support." The 10 of Spades, Terrene, is compatible with the Jack of Hearts both in suit and in age. Additionally, we know that Earth provides stability for the otherwise formless Water, and that Terrene symbolizes many nurturing characteristics.

I continued. "There are also less prominent but positive relationships with males, peers of M. Friendships are very important to your son." This spread was quite remarkable in that there were so many young court figures, which gave a clear picture of the very social fraternity environment.

Mrs. H confided that all I had said seemed very true, and that the female spoken of was surely M's girlfriend. I told her that they were a wonderful match and could even be married someday. Mrs. H said she had thought this before.

At this point in the reading there was a good rapport established with the client, and it was time to get to the crux of her concern, glaringly represented by the "Sword of Destruction." Speaking again, I said,

"There is a very strong force with your son right now. It is pictured as a sword. He will use this energy to cut away the past and the life he had as a youth. This will help him to pass into manhood. It is important. Like any powerful tool, the sword is also a weapon, one that he will learn to control in time." This interpretation of the 7 of Spades was supported by the harmonious environment of the spread. Remember, the negative potentials of cards do not manifest in positive surroundings. I reassured Mrs. H that what her son was going through was normal and healthy, and that although there could be more rebellious behavior to come, it did not look like it would escalate into anything serious. Mrs. H thanked me for the reading.

THE BULLET

"THE BULLET" IS ANOTHER WAY OF SAYING "cutting a card" and is named for its ability to get to the core of an issue quickly and directly. The technique is rather self-explanatory. After focusing on the question at hand, cut into the deck and see what you get. Sometimes I will cut several "bullets" while listening to a person speak rather than do a layout or in addition to a layout. This is one of my favorites for telephone readings. I will simply open the deck from time to time as the person is speaking and glance at whatever card is exposed. In this way, a card dialogue occurs, a silent and moving reflection of the words being spoken.

Because any single card possesses a variety of possible meanings, the bullet technique does present a bit of a handicap. Cards laid out as part of a spread can be seen and interpreted in the context of a larger environment. Bullets are solitary messengers. If you don't understand the meaning that a given card has on the question or situation, that's okay. Resist at all costs the temptation of asking the same question again in hopes of receiving something that makes more sense. The absence of an immediate interpretation simply means you are on the brink of having a breakthrough, a new understanding of the language the cards speak. If it helps, you can always ask the powers that be for clarification. You can even take the card received as a bullet and make it your assigned card in a Lost Man Spread in order to observe it as part of a bigger picture.

The Geomantic Layout

ANOTHER OPTION IS TO USE YOUR CARDS TO FORM THE SHAPES of geomantic figures. Making symbols out of cards creates very aesthetically pleasing spreads. The figure of Acquisitio, for example, would look like this:

ACQUISITIO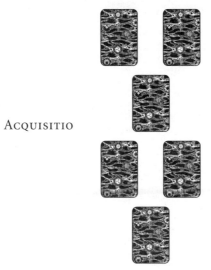

Begin by turning the cards for the top line, then follow with the Throat, Torso, and finally the Foot position cards. When two cards share a line, lay the right card down first. In the case of Acquisitio, the order would be:

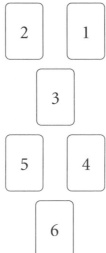

You can turn your cards off the top of the deck following the shuffle, or you can even cut into the deck as in the *Cat Spread*, count your piles of four to get a time in the future, and then turn your cards for the figure.

To determine which of the sixteen geomantic figures to lay out, select the one that best symbolizes the situation in question. A divorce, for example, could be represented by either Amissio or "The Dragon's Tail." A new love could be depicted as Conjunctio, Acquisitio, "The Dragon's Head" or even the two figures of Puer and Puella (the boy and girl) together. Ask your intuition. You can also use this layout to clarify a geomantic figure already received in a 4- or 16-card reading.

In interpreting your layout, remember that each separate line of the figure corresponds to one of the four card positions, as explained in *The Significance of Card Positions* (p. 119). Two cards on a line work together to define whatever that position represents.

THE BRIDGE LAYOUT

THIS IS A PICTURE LAYOUT that gives you a general look at the energies at play in a person's life. Before shuffling, locate the 6 of Clubs ("The Bridge") within your deck and lay it face up on the table. Now have the person you are reading for mix the cards and turn one off the top of the deck for each of the four sides of "The Bridge." These can be laid out in whichever order feels right intuitively. The card to the left of "The Bridge" represents the past or what you are leaving behind. The card to the right is what is to come. Above symbolizes what is on The Bridge, for example, what is currently being manifested or carried with you across The Bridge. The card at the bottom shows what is underneath The Bridge, in other words, what is being transcended. This is the fodder for transformation, the situations which must be overcome in order to change the conditions of the past into the promises of the future.

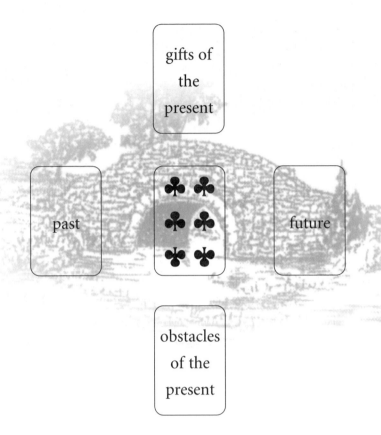

LOST AND FOUND

I LOVE IT WHEN I COME ACROSS A RANDOM PLAYING CARD. To me, it has no less meaning than anything I would get from a good reading; in fact, sometimes it has more. The difference with cards found on a sidewalk or a kitchen floor is that they are given, not asked for. They are messages--whisperings from the unseen, appearing at those times when Providence deems it so.

Some of my greatest insights into the meanings of the playing cards and the way they can behave have come from those tossed or lost by a stranger. Also, I have found that the information given does not always pertain directly to the person receiving it. Cards can reflect the person or place from which they came. For example, I can recall walking into the living room of a couple who was going through a very tough separation only to see the 2 of Spades laying face up on the floor—a reflection of what was going on in their lives, not mine.

Cards that suddenly flip out of the deck while being shuffled for a reading are another aspect of this same phenomenon. You didn't ask for them yet there they are. They want to be noticed. I always make a mental note of cards that appear in this way, then put them back in the deck with the rest of their card friends. It's a real mind blower when the same card then reappears as part of the layout, as it sometimes will. This is a message that is literally shouting at you.

Once you learn the language of the playing cards, no card is really ever "random" anymore, never "accidental." It has meaning, something to say. What we are studying is a universal language, a language of color, number, and archetypal image. Playing cards are part of cultures across the globe, found in homes in Paraguay, Portugal, and Paris. They span epochs in history, the reaches of centuries. Once you start thinking "in cards," you plug in to a broad, mystical network. Channels open and communication begins.

Final Frontiers

PART FOUR will point the direction to places you can enter only alone: the realms of your own inner being. Words can dance only on the brink of those things that must be experienced to be understood. Ideas on the vast and very personal art of intuition are followed by the introduction to the master spread, the Reading of Seasons.

On $Intuition$

NNER KNOWING OR "INTUITION" is already part of you. It is
here right now and has been all along. It's just waiting for you to
join with it, to reclaim it. It is eternally patient, there as soon as you are.
You probably already have an inkling of what brings you closer to this
part of yourself. The pages in this chapter contain a sampling of my own
ideas and experiences with intuition. Take what you will. Follow the yel-
low brick road.

THE REFLECTIVE WORLD

EVERY TIME I LAY OUT THE CARDS, I am captured by their magic. For
me, each reading is proof positive that there are unrealized and exciting
possibilities within the human being. If we are paying attention, we will
find that the world around us is continually supplying messages that are
meant to assist us, answer our questions, guide us on our way. When we
handle the cards, they, too, become part of our environment and, as
such, reflect what we need to know at that moment. We are electric,
magnetic, and dynamic beings, and we attract as well as affect our surroundings.

Have you ever turned on the radio only to find that the words to a
song provided exactly what you needed to hear at the time? If so, then
you are already "tuning in" to this phenomenon. I often enjoy doing
card readings in noisy places, as I will pick up relevant words or phrases
wafting my way from random voices in the crowd or from music that is
playing. The cards are just one part of what I am paying attention to.

Carl Jung noticed these occurrences in his own life and talked about them in his theory called Synchronicity. Socrates was also well aware of it and relied on messages from the world around him for daily guidance. When questioned about the origin of the messages, he declined comment, saying only that they were "Divine Somethings."

As we begin to understand the world as a place that is responsive to who we are, the magic of how the cards work begins to unfold. Instead of an unexplainable mystery, a right-on-target reading appears as a natural occurrence, as natural as seeing one's reflection in a pool of water.

Readings that miss the mark, so to speak, need not become a source of despair. They are one of your most valuable teachers. Usually it is our own interpretation of the information given that is the source of error. Also keep in mind that because the cards function reflectively, in some instances the person receiving the reading may be blocking information from coming through with their own skepticism or closed-off attitude. Believe it or not, sometimes people ask questions they really do not wish to know the answer to. The cards cannot act against a person's will.

THE PAUSE

WHEN DOING READINGS, there are certain techniques or practices that will bring you closer to your intuition and sharpen your skills as a reader. First of all, remember it is not really necessary (or desirable) to try and read all of the possible information within a given spread. Not all things have equal importance. The main messages have a way of jumping out at you. Over-analysis can kill a good reading and detract from what is important.

Secondly: Use silence. Resist the temptation of speaking just to fill space. After saying something of significance, stop. Take a deep breath. Look into the eyes of the person sitting across from you and simply affirm your connection. Yes, right in the middle of the reading.

When you are busy chatting, it is nearly impossible to hear the inner voice. Speaking puts you into a part of your brain not necessarily conducive to sensitivity. Quiet evokes a certain communication beyond words. It opens you to the magic of the moment and gives weight and power to the words you do say. I once heard a quote from a composer who said, "It's not the notes, but the spaces between, that determine the music."

LEARNING TO TRUST

A NUMBER OF CARD READERS, reportedly using their card correspondences dogmatically, have been stricken with the dreaded Dogma Breath, a foul smelling odor reminiscent of canine exhalations that drives away clients and others. Take heed!

All joking aside, when learning any new skill, it takes a certain amount of time and experience before it becomes natural, before you incorporate it into your being. As such, your readings may feel a bit stiff or disjointed in the beginning. You may have to rely heavily on memorized meanings. This is natural and to be expected. Don't give up on yourself. In time you will form your own relationship with the cards, opening the way for intuition to enter.

In many ways, reading a spread of cards can be compared to reading a page of music. All the notes and scales that have been practiced and studied allow the fingers to move confidently from note to note until something greater actually enters in. Soon a feeling for the composition begins to emerge and the music transcends the ink on the page. In the same way, the cards will reveal to you how they want to be interpreted each time. Let each reading be new. Remain the student and become the master. Here I think it will be helpful as well as entertaining to illustrate with a true story.

On long hot summer afternoons, years ago, Lainy would let me sit at a table near her as she read her cards for customers in the marketplace. Lainy was grand entertainment and drew a steady stream of clientele. This was a woman who had a very unique way of looking at the world and at cards. She was a master at certain self-discovered card reading techniques, one of which she talked about as "waiting for something to float up."

So, one day after a young woman had seated herself for a reading, Lainy was looking over the spread of cards and what caught her attention was a button pictured on the clothing of one of the card characters and the fact that it was undone. This must have been what "floated up" out of the spread because Lainy exclaimed, "My goodness, you're coming undone!" No sooner had these words been spoken than the woman burst into tears, confessing she felt her whole life was "coming undone."

The moral of this story is use your intuition. Dare to give it a chance. The most you have to lose is Dogma Breath.

GROUNDING

And God said to Moses, "Take off your shoes, because the ground where you are standing is Holy Ground."
                              —Exodus 3:5

GROUNDING IS A POINT THAT CAN HARDLY BE OVER-EMPHASIZED. As a reader, or any serious student of the psychic arts, it is vital to fortify your connection to the Earth.

Concerning this topic, my favorite analogy is the tree. A tree's roots must grow strong and deep so its branches can aspire skyward. The upward growth and the downward growth must occur simultaneously. The roots provide nourishment from the Earth and protect the tree from uprooting as its growing limbs reach ever higher.

We can take this analogy and apply it directly to ourselves. Your physical body is composed of the Element Earth and constitutes your grounding system, your roots. The more subtle mental and emotional bodies can be compared to your heavenly-reaching branches. By strengthening the connection to your physical presence, you fortify your roots and support the growth of psychic abilities.

Often the temptation for people who are sensitive to psychic energies is to neglect the physical. We probably all know someone who frequently gets "spaced out." Maybe that someone is you. This can actually be identified in a spread of cards by a lack of Spades along with an overabundance of Hearts or Clubs or both. Spades correspond to the physical body and Hearts and Clubs correspond to the emotional and mental bodies, respectively. The problem with this lack of grounding is that it is nearly guaranteed to produce imaginary experience disconnected from reality. As discussed in the section titled *Generating Suit Energies*, each of the four suits represents a necessary part of a healthy psychology. Balance is power! Grounding keeps your psychic explorations connected and relevant to the here and now.

There are so many ways to ground yourself. You can really be creative and have fun with this. The basic idea is to energize or bring attention to the experience of your own body and its relationship with the Earth. If you haven't already, try incorporating a regular practice that supports this. Routine in itself is conducive to grounding. Remember, regularity and discipline are Spade characteristics. Tailor your grounding program to fit your individual lifestyle. Yoga and relaxation exercises are excellent practices for increasing your physical awareness. Hiking, biking, dancing, gardening, even cleaning the house, also work to support groundedness. Performing your activities with a quiet attention will multiply your results.

Eating food is another way we commune with the Earth. Eating styles reveal a lot about how grounded we are. Do your meals occur on a regular schedule or are you a hit-or-miss eater? Do you eat standing up, while driving the car, or watching TV? Are you drawn more toward empty-calorie foods or healthy, wholesome foods? Interestingly enough, the times I find myself overeating coincide with the times when I have a real need for grounding. This seems to be my body's unconscious attempt to bring me back down to Earth. As an experiment, prepare a luscious meal of root foods like potatoes, carrots, onions, etc., and see how it makes you feel (see recipe at the end of this section). As you eat, be conscious of what you are doing. Once again, attention multiplies the value of the experience.

The time during a reading is obviously key for grounding. Be aware of sensations occurring in your body and allow yourself to become relaxed. I like to keep both feet flat on the floor, and I have the person I'm reading for do the same. The soles of the feet are what good old Mom Nature made for putting on her. The study of reflexology reveals how each part of the body is energetically linked to a specific part of the foot. When you touch your feet to the Earth, you energize your whole body with Earth vibrations.

As an exercise, visualize sending very strong, very alive roots out the bottoms of your feet. Send them down deep into dark, rich Earth. Feel yourself firmly rooted, firmly connected and supported. Feel perfect nourishment entering the cells of your body. Now expand your experience to include your skyward reaching branches, like hundreds of ethereal fingertips sprouting upward and outward above the crown of your head. Feel them as soft and green, even effervescent. They are fed by your connection to the Earth. Penetrate the sky. Absorb radiant sunlight. Be filled with cosmic energy.

 ## Terrene's Roasted Roots

PREHEAT OVEN TO 425°

3	carrots	¼	cup of olive oil
2	large beets	⅛	cup of balsamic vinegar
2	russet potatoes		or soy sauce
2	parsnips	6	cloves of garlic mashed
2	onions		salt and pepper to taste
1½	pound rutabaga		herbs of choice
1	large sweet potato		

Cut all vegetables into smallish size chunks, less than 1". Combine olive oil, vinegar or soy sauce, garlic, salt and pepper, and any herbs of choice. Pour over veggies and transfer to a roasting pan or cookie sheet. (Line with foil for a nice cleanup.)

Roast on top shelf of the oven for about 30 minutes, stirring one or two times until they are tender and browned. Makes four servings.

Best eaten with shoes removed.

READING THE CARDS FOR YOURSELF

READING FOR YOURSELF CAN BE A GOOD WAY to get to know your deck and increase your understanding of how it works, but it can also spell tricky business. Because your deck is so readily available, it is easy to overuse, easy to become overly reliant on the messages given. Remember always that the cards are a tool only. The magic is in *you*. Without you, the cards are lifeless and meaningless pieces of paper. Their beauty lies in their ability to point us back to ourselves, back to our own intuition and what we already know but simply cannot see. Overuse constitutes what I call badgering the cards and negates the power of what you are doing.

You can think of consulting with your deck as consulting with a wise and venerable elder. Once an answer is given, it is received very graciously, with reverence. You would not show disrespect by asking the same question again or tire the elder person with too many concerns. In order to advance in this line of work, we must trust in what we are given and know that sometimes the understanding or acceptance of that answer follows later. We must find comfort in realizing that there is a greater plan for us all, superceding our own shortsighted self-interests.

One more thing to consider when thinking about this topic: There is a certain level of energy created by two people that is more difficult to attain by yourself. Reading for someone else or having someone else read for you arouses something special, something palpably different than being alone. Also, the information received is potentially more objective simply because it comes from someone outside of you. When you read for yourself you typically have an emotional investment in the question. That's why you are asking it. Another person provides an impartial channel. Messages given are less likely to get tangled up with your own hopes and expectations.

Consider carefully when choosing whether or not to read for yourself. Don't let your practice become a crutch. Be selective about when to consult your deck, and your cards will give voice to the wise spirit that lives inside you.

The Reading of Seasons

*T*HIS READING MAKES USE of the same fundamental concepts introduced in the 4-card spread, but expands it all to include sixteen cards and twelve geomantic figures. It forecasts a year of time, the entire scope of the playing card calendar. In many ways, it is the culmination of the ideas in this book.

As we have learned, the playing deck is a magical instrument, a microcosmic reflection of our world. The Reading of Seasons works in harmony with this knowledge, allowing you to explore the mystical potential of your cards in a practical way. It is complex, like the deck itself, and requires time and dedication for its secrets to spread their wings before you. If you feel you have a good working knowledge of the previous sections of the text and are looking for something more, this reading is for you. If you are dabbling with the ideas, you really don't need a spread this involved.

I use the magical suit names when performing this reading. Just the sound of these words as they roll off the tongue seems to invoke the spirit of the cards, the wisdom of the Elements, rising from ancient tombs.

LAYING OUT THE CARDS

AFTER YOUR DECK HAS BEEN PREPARED BY THE SHUFFLE, divide it into four equal piles of thirteen cards. This is done by counting cards in your hand from the top of the deck downward, making sure not to rearrange them in any way as you do. This means that the card that is on top of the deck after the shuffle becomes the card on top of the first pile. As you make your piles, arrange them in order from right to left, as shown below (Illustration A).

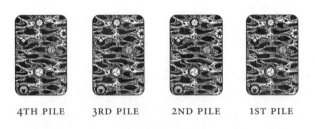

4TH PILE   3RD PILE   2ND PILE   1ST PILE

ILLUSTRATION A

Each stack of thirteen represents one season of our year, thirteen weeks. The pile on the right is *Ignita*, and corresponds to the Autumnal cycle. The second pile from the right is *Ethra*, the season of Summer. The third stack of thirteen is *Agana*, the Spring, and the Fourth pile is *Terra*, the cycle of hibernation, or Winter.

Proceed by turning the first four cards off of each pile, exactly as in the 4-card spread. These cards will stand as representatives for each of the seasons. The remaining nine cards in each pile remain unseen, their faces turned to the table. You now have sixteen cards to view in the shape of a square, a perfect four-by-four configuration (Illustration B).

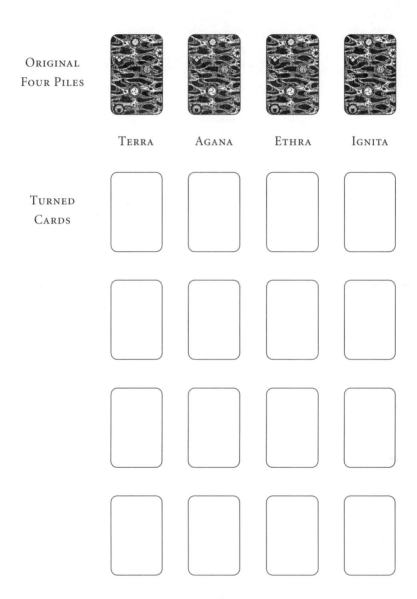

ORIGINAL
FOUR PILES

TERRA   AGANA   ETHRA   IGNITA

TURNED
CARDS

ILLUSTRATION B

DISSECTING THE LAYOUT

$\mathcal{A}$nd thus everie pricke signifieth a Starre,
and everie line an Element and everie
figure the faure quarters of the world . . .
—Christopher Cattan, 1658, Italy

IN EXAMINING THIS PECULIAR QUOTATION written four full centuries
ago, the secrets of the Reading of Seasons begin to unfold. In his best-
selling work, *The Geomancie of Maister Christopher Cattan*, the Italian
scholar expounds on a system of divination that corresponds in many
ways to the 16-card layout and its ultimate conversion into geomantic
figures.

The "pricke" Cattan speaks of refers to the odd or even "starre" that
each of the cards becomes as we translate the numbers and colors into
their geomantic or binary counterparts. For Cattan and his contempo-
raries, geomancy was considered an art reflecting the will of the heavens, and so, appropriately, stars were adopted over the dots or lines
formerly used to inscribe the figures. Each geomantic figure thus
appears as a heavenly cluster, and a group of figures together becomes a
whole sky of twinkling luminaries.

The next portion of the sentence, "and everie line an Element," corresponds to the horizontally observed rows within the layout
(Illustration C). Each of these rows signifies a suit and accordingly, an
Element. As in the 4-card spread, they also signify a part of the body.
Following the same technique as previously learned, mentally relate all
questions to one (or more) suit category. Your answer will be found in
the respective horizontal line. Learn to observe the world through the
looking glass of Fire, Air, Water, and Earth. A money question will be
referred to the Head line, a housing question to the Foot line, etc.
Because there are now four cards for each position rather than one (as
in the 4-card spread), broader and more detailed responses are possible.

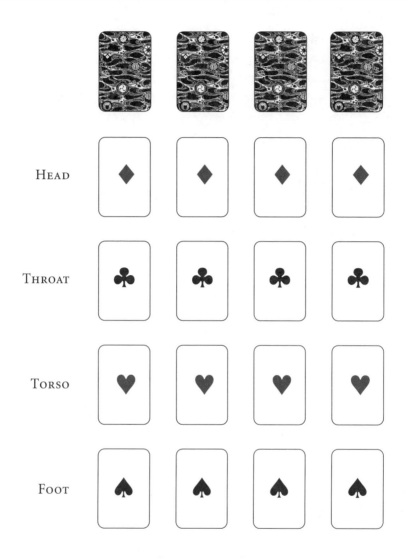

ILLUSTRATION C

Moving now to the final words of Cattan's quote, "and everie figure the faure quarters of the world," we stumble on a major difference between this reading and the junior size. Looking at the vertical rows within our layout, we see that not only does each form a complete figure, consisting of a Head, Throat, Torso, and Foot, but also represents a *season* and a *direction* as well (Illustration D); in other words, "the

faure quarters of the world." This gives the exciting possibility of track-
ing the person who is being read over the passage of time, the turning
of seasons. Issues and questions are seen in movement. Each vertical line
is read just as you would read a 4-card spread, one for each season of the
year. The directional correspondences of South, East, West, and North
can give locational advice if needed.

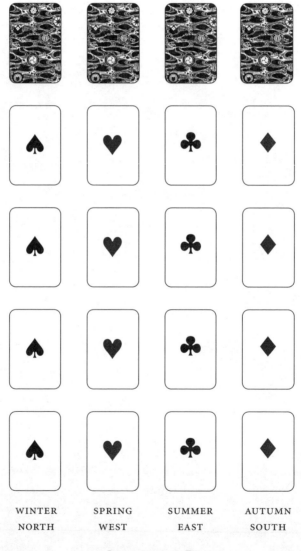

WINTER   SPRING   SUMMER   AUTUMN

NORTH   WEST   EAST   SOUTH

ILLUSTRATION D

Notice how the order of seasons as observed from right to left is in keeping with the Diamond/Club/Heart/Spade sequence used throughout the book. Now reverse this direction and what do you see? The seasons appear in the exact order we experience them in nature: Winter ushers in the New Year, Spring comes next, followed by Summer, and finally Autumn.

Having explored both horizontal and vertical lines, the next step is to *combine* these two fundamental rows of correspondence. In doing so we find a very special diagonal row, a third dimension of possibility.

Looking at the figure shown in Illustration E, the cards appear much

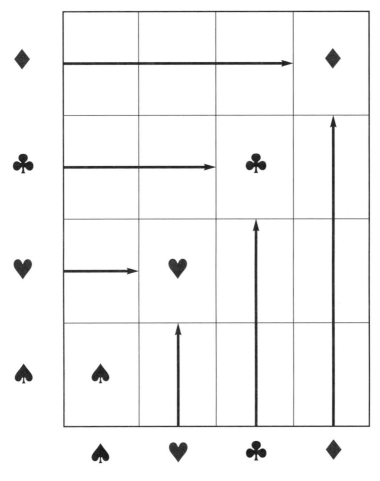

ILLUSTRATION E

like a graph. Viewing your spread in this way can help you become aware of patterns and relationships existing within it. Beginning at the top right corner where the two Ignita (Diamond) rows of correspondence intersect, and traveling diagonally to the bottom left corner where the two Terra (Spade) lines meet, you have a key group of card positions. Together they form a pathway, the "core journey" of the reading.

Each card in this row is in the central position for one of the four suits and holds additional importance for this reason. Keep this in mind as you are interpreting the horizontal and vertical rows of correspondence, as each contains one. They are primary messages, the axis of the spread.

THE MYSTIC SQUARE

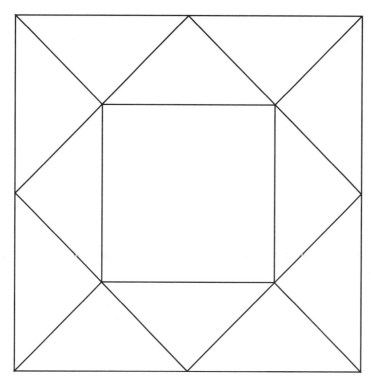

This
quandrous
query
of lines
and leary
makes me
feary,
my deary.

—AC

ILLUSTRATION F

THE MYSTIC SQUARE (Illustration F) is used to house the information collected in The Reading of Seasons. Once complete, it provides a source of reference for future study, much like an astrological chart. The figure itself dates back many centuries and can be found in early European divinatory-type manuscripts. Its elegant construction of three perfect squares placed one within the other yields a design beautiful in its simplicity and symmetry. The natural formation of twelve triangular divisions in addition to the centermost square gives a total of thirteen sections, a number of grand importance in the playing deck, as we well know. Among other things, the Mystic Square is a compass, the four sides of which pertain to the four directions. For this reason, it is fitting when casting a chart to align the top of your page with true North.

FILLING IN THE CHART

LOOKING AT THE SIXTEEN CARDS LAID OUT, write the number and suit of each in the innermost square of the chart. These notations are known as card "signatures." Write them in the exact positions in which they appear on the table. This gives you a record of the spread for future reference and allows you to calculate your geomantic figures on the Mystic Square without having to look back and forth from cards to paper.

Focusing now on the vertical lines of the layout and recalling what we've already learned about calculating geomancy, we can proceed to fill in the remaining sections. Remember that a vertical column of cards produces three geomantic figures: one derived by number, one by color, and one by the combination of the other two. These are the Witnesses and the Judge, respectively. Because these vertical rows "give birth" to the geomantic figures, they are referred to as Mothers. In the Reading of Seasons, there are four: the Diamond or *Ignita* Mother, the Club or *Ethra* Mother, the Heart or *Agana* Mother, and the Spade or *Terra* Mother. Each Mother has her own quadrant of the Mystic Square to call home, conveniently divided into three rooms, one for each of her geomantic children (Illustration G).

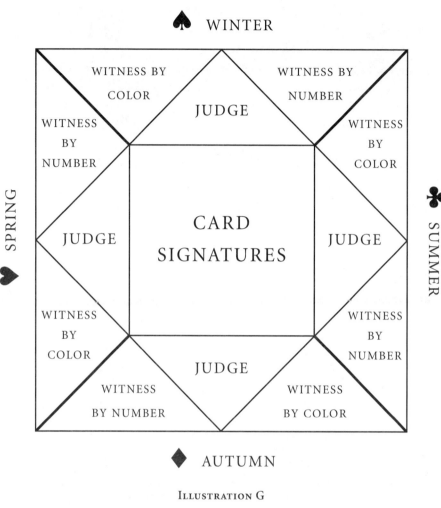

♠ WINTER

WITNESS BY COLOR

WITNESS BY NUMBER

JUDGE

WITNESS BY NUMBER

WITNESS BY COLOR

SPRING ♥

☘ SUMMER

CARD SIGNATURES

JUDGE

JUDGE

WITNESS BY COLOR

WITNESS BY NUMBER

JUDGE

WITNESS BY NUMBER

WITNESS BY COLOR

♦ AUTUMN

ILLUSTRATION G

Beginning with the Ignita Mother, draw your figures in the Southern section of the chart, then proceed with Ethra, Agana, and Terra, but with one significant change from the way you have previously learned. Instead of using the top card as the color indicator when determining your second Witness, use the card from the diagonal row of key card positions. Only the Ignita Mother will use the top card as color indicator, as that is the key card for this line.

Notice how the positions for the number and color witnesses

alternate as you move around the periphery of the square. The number witnesses are all placed in the right hand positions and the color witnesses on the left *as if you were standing in the center of the chart.* This is important, as the two Witnesses have direct correlation to the right and left sides of the body (as discussed on p. 165). Take care not to rotate the page as you fill in the chart, as geomantic figures change meaning when viewed upside-down.

The innermost square of geomantic signatures features all four of the Judges and is known as the Square of Judgment. Looking at it gives you a geomantic summation of the year in question. Illustration H shows the Mystic Square filled in with a sample spread, complete with the geomantic planetary rulers.

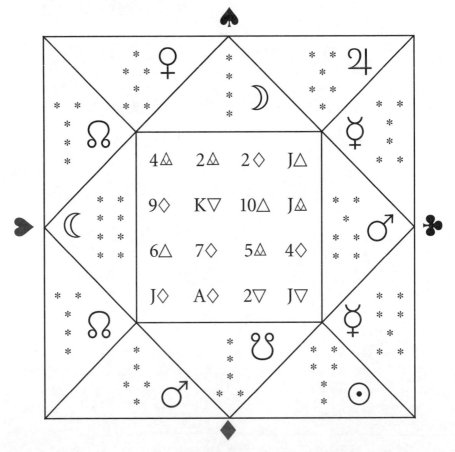

ILLUSTRATION H

Here you will see a shorthand method for writing the suit signs. I find it to be much quicker and less awkward than drawing the standard figures. The shorthand shown is: ♦ = ◇, ♣ = △, ♥ = ▽, and ♠ = △.

Shorthand for Writing Suit Signs

♦ = ◇

♣ = △

♥ = ▽

♠ = △

All in all, the Reading of Seasons may seem a little complex, and truly it is. But, as stated previously, complexity allows for accuracy and depth in a reading. It also offers the serious reader something to grow into. With a little practice you'll be humming through the charting portion of this layout with ease.

A SAMPLE READING

USING THE LAYOUT SHOWN IN ILLUSTRATION H, let's walk through a sample interpretation of the Reading of Seasons. It's a good idea to actually lay this spread out with your own cards so you can refer to them as you read along.

Before looking at individual rows of cards, it is useful to view the spread as a whole in order to get some general impressions. One of the most immediate things I notice about this spread is that there is a fairly balanced show of black and red cards and that they are interspersed nicely throughout the reading. This points to a healthy interplay between the outer and inner life of the individual. Another thing that gets my attention is that there are lots of Jacks, in fact, all four. Knowing what we do about the general nature of the Jack personality, we can say that this person has a very fun-loving, youthful spirit. Because court cards represent actual people, there is also likely to be a number of young males in his or her life.

Because Jacks so strongly dominate the court scene, I would suspect that this person possesses what you could call a Peter Pan complex. In other words, they're not really convinced they want to join the adult world. But before making a strong statement like that, it is always a good idea to look for other evidence in the layout that supports it. In the given instance, we find plenty.

First of all, there is a notable lack of court figures who are able to exert any real authority. The only card of higher rank than a Jack is the King of Hearts, a party-loving guy with a big heart. This is not a King who keeps others in line.

Secondly, we see that there are not many Spades in this layout. This suit has the least number of cards overall and also happens to symbolize discipline and responsibility. The presence of four Jacks along with the absence of an authority figure and the low number of Spades is enough to safely rest our Peter Pan syndrome case.

Continuing on with the initial evaluation of this layout, something very interesting jumps out from the key diagonal line of cards: a vital alliance between Pampero, the Jack of Spades, and Terrene, the Lady of Spades. These two are natural mates and represent the strongest partnership in this spread. Together they symbolize many down-to-earth traits along with a reliability possessed by few cards of such youthful status, the significance of which is further heightened by their placement within the diagonal line. So, in spite of some of the more juvenile Jackish traits we have seen, there is a core awareness on a more mature level that in time may penetrate this person's life in a greater way.

Because the Spade Lady and Jack are separated by time (one appears in the Autumn line and the other in Summer), I would venture to say these people are apart somehow. Since vertical lines also symbolize directions of the compass, this is likely to entail distance. These two could be sometime lovers, brother and sister, or long-distance best friends. I also get that the depth of their relationship is kind of secret, a rather private affair. They probably feel like they are alone in a storm, so to speak—the solitary rock on a windswept shore, the only real sign of stability in the layout.

At this point, an overall feeling for the spread has emerged, and we can proceed to the individual rows of correspondence, illuminating separate areas of the person's life more fully. I like to begin with the horizontal rows, touching on each of the four areas represented and follow up with an interpretation of the vertical rows and how they relate to the geomancy. Since the completed reading typically takes a full hour,

I will provide here only a limited selection of correspondences, choosing those I feel will be most helpful to the reader.

Looking first at the Foot line or bottommost horizontal row, we glimpse a picture of this person's life as it relates to the suit of Spades. Here we find the Jack of Diamonds and the Jack of Hearts, the Ace of Diamonds and the Deuce of Hearts: all red. This intense mixture of the Fire and Water Elements spells volatility and impulsiveness. Applying this to the Spade domain of occupation, we see that this is the kind of. person who needs to change jobs often or have a profession that involves lots of excitement and opportunity to be creative, emotional, and spontaneous, such as an entertainment career of some kind. Because the Ace of Diamonds is in this row, it also indicates a strong will to succeed and make money even in the absence of strong work ethics. Another dynamic not to be overlooked exists between the Deuce of Hearts and the two Jacks. This little trio of cards hanging out on the line associated with Earth reveals the nature of relationship for this person. Here we see physical, sexual love as opposed to heart-centered love. This is further supported by the fact that no Heart cards or personality cards show up at all on the horizontal Heart line above. In this spread, La Hire and Dango are players, a role they assume quite naturally. For this person, love is more about physical passion than anything that touches the heart; at least that is what is being projected for the next year.

Although there is much of interest in the Heart line, for the sake of being brief, I will point out only that which relates to the key Heart line card, the 7 of Diamonds. This is an interesting placement for the "Sword of Truth," telling of a direct honesty with oneself and others concerning matters of the heart and soul. So, even with the unwillingness or inability to experience emotional depth, as further revealed by the accompanying cards on this line, the person has the honorable trait of being up front about it.

Moving to the Throat line, the line associated with Clubs, we find the highest numbered cards of any row and an equal representation of suit signs. This is a place of power for the person being read, an area where he/she shines. Here there is an interesting relationship between the King of Hearts and the Lady of Spades (cards of compatible suits), as well as the notable presence of the magical Jack, Lancelot, and the good Knight, Gawain. This person has a lot of social contacts and a real talent when it comes to communication and connecting with people on the level of ideas. Tying this together with what we already know about this person's affinity for the entertainment profession and their ability to be up front when it comes to matters of the heart, it is easy to see that they would make a great public presence, a natural on the radio or stage.

Ascending now to the uppermost row, we find the two Deuces crying out for attention. As previously covered (see *More on Numbers*, p. 135), any number that repeats itself speaks to the need for the lessons of that number to be learned. Because there are actually three Deuces in this layout, this becomes one of the central messages conveyed by this reading. Situations calling for a greater level of cooperation and an ability to put oneself in another's shoes, so to speak, will be a recurring theme for this person. Since the Head line deals specifically with issues related to one's identity and to finances, we can also say that this person's character is defined in many ways by their competitive nature (2 of Diamonds). We see that financial resources will remain reasonably stable (remember the characteristics of the Jack of Spades) but probably will not meet this person's expectations, as most of the numbers in this row are quite low and the 4 of Clubs, as we know, is a card symbolizing slow energies and lessons in the art of patience.

Switching gears now, let's look at the vertical rows of correspondence and how they relate to the geomancy. This is the part of the reading where time enters in. I usually begin with the season in which the reading is taking place and proceed from there. As the solstices and equinoxes that determine the seasons vary slightly from year to year, it is good to check in with your calendar so you know when these cycles occur. Approximate dates of the seasons are:

Winter:	December 22nd to March 20th
Spring:	March 21st to June 21st
Summer:	June 22nd to September 22nd
Autumn:	September 23rd to December 21st

For example's sake, let's say that September 1st is the date of the reading we are currently interpreting. This puts us in the season of Summer, which correlates with the second vertical row from the right, the Ethra Mother. We'll make this our starting point and cycle through the seasons one by one until we come back around to the present. Again, I'll move rather quickly, highlighting the more obvious correspondences. Details are best clarified in the presence of the person being read, where your connection can aid your intuition.

Looking at our four cards, we see again two Deuces in addition to Terrene and the "Wind Cape." The geomancy for this section of the layout is found in the eastern quadrant of the Mystic Square, with Albus and Conjunctio as the Witnesses and Rubeus as the Judge. Anytime Rubeus appears, it is a signal to sit up and take note, or more precisely, take warning.

Using the information indicated by the cards, we see Terrene playing a major role in the current events. Not only is she the only personality card, but she is also in the key position for this row. The two red Deuces appearing in the upper and lower positions give me the feeling of sitting on a seesaw, a this-way-then-that-way game perpetuated by the confusion going on in the Heart position. You can even see a picture of a seesaw in the formation of stars that make Conjunctio. Rubeus often points to emotions bubbling up to the surface from way down deep — down where we've stuffed or hidden them, hoping they'll just go away. I sense a great amount of discomfort here.

Moving on to the time of year that is about to unfold for this person, we look to the vertical row on the far right, the Ignita Mother. Because of all the court cards, we can say that the Fall will be a very socially oriented time. When Jacks mingle with the playful energy of The South Wind, you can be sure there will be lots of lighthearted, prankish behavior. All of this young male energy is nicely mirrored in the geomancy with Puer as the first Witness. The second Witness (Fortuna Major), the Witness corresponding to the emotional experience of the situation, shows that this environment will support this person to feel comfortable, to feel themselves, to shine. Again as before, the Judge (Cauda Draconis) is an unfortunate one, and happy results still elude this person.

Skipping across the layout now to the far left and the Terra Mother, we'll take a look at Winter. In this phase of the year, I get that it will be necessary for the person to seek out those things that give personal inspiration, a time to focus on themselves and what makes them tick. This is reflected in the spread by the two high-numbered Diamond cards, a suit representing concerns of the ego. Because Diamonds are also associated with light and heat, it might be a good time of year to get out of the cold weather and go somewhere warmer. If the person already lives in a warm climate, they might want to consider taking a trip that would benefit them personally, provide enlightening experiences and inspiration. The figure of Via in the seat of the Judge, as well as the presence of "The East Wind" in the top dog position, further confirms that this indeed would be an auspicious time to do some traveling.

At last we come to the Spring, the time furthest from the date of the reading, and we actually see some real resolution to the rather disconcerting situations of the previous seasons. The geomancy is very encouraging with "The Head of the Dragon" (Caput Draconis), a figure indicating new and fortunate beginnings, appearing in both Witness positions. Populus as the Judge simply reflects the figures from which it came, in this case an affirmation of good things.

Remembering what has been covered in the section titled *Further Geomantic Indications* (p. 168), we can see that the Deuce of Clubs is auspiciously placed in the position that takes on additional significance in relation to the two Witnesses. This card reveals the nature of the new beginning for this person. As we know, "The Friends" symbolizes some of the more mellow manifestations of the number Two and in this case I feel it represents peace within the individual. This Deuce also happens to be in compatible suit with the key card in this line, the 7 of Diamonds, indicating peace within oneself that is in harmony with truth and fed by the desire to live in accordance with this law. At this point, it seems that the much-needed lessons of the number Two have been largely integrated and this person is ready to begin the next cycle of seasons on a new threshold.

In Closing

M Y PARTING AND MOST FUNDAMENTAL piece of advice is don't give up on yourself. Spend time with your deck. Pour a glass of wine, light a candle, and lay out cards. Practice on family and friends who will be forgiving and remember to be forgiving of yourself, too. A little insecurity is just a growing pain.

Ultimately, a reading is an act of grace, an affirmation of the wisdom in all things. This is probably why I love this art so much and also why I wrote this book. Sharing the experience multiplies the satisfaction. May your efforts be returned to you in blessings never imagined.

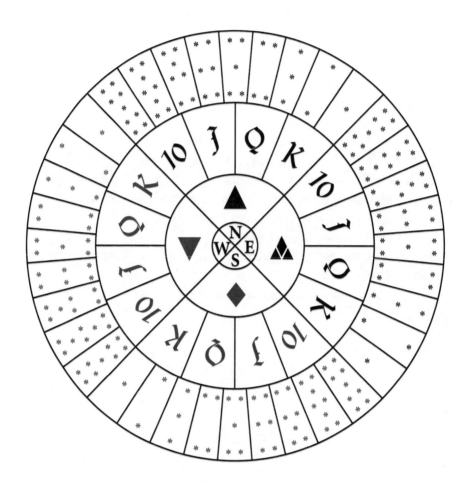

MANDALA OF THE PLAYING CARD DECK
The 52 cards and their quadrants, a harmonic view.
Illustration by Ana Cortez.

Book Two

Book Two

ESSAYS, NOTES, AND
COMMENTARY ON

The

Playing Card Oracles

BY

C. J. Freeman

INTRODUCTION BY
Ana Cortez

Introduction

A THOUSAND THANK-YOUS TO MY FATHER, C.J. Freeman, for
this very generous addition to *The Playing Card Oracles*.
Playing card history is a subject in which I am admittedly non-versed.
For my dad, however, it seems only to feed a near insatiable appetite.
The research he has done in this area has served as a guiding beacon in
our work together, as our intention was never to reinvent but rather to
resurrect what lay in the deck. My dad has been like a conveniently
located encyclopedia of playing card factoids, as close as my own
telephone.

This portion of the book is invaluable for the simple reason that
much confusion, misinformation, and basic blankness abounds
regarding the origin of the cards. To quote my father, "I dare say, there
is probably nothing with such widespread cultural significance we
know less about than the playing cards." His treatment of this very
lengthy and rather tangled subject is unique — dotted with anecdotes
and sprinkled with academia, topped with a little theoretical spice. It
caters to a perhaps more select audience than Book One, but for those
who are so inclined, it is here. The time line that follows provides a
more abbreviated version of playing card history.

—AC

$\mathcal{S}$ignificant $\mathcal{D}$ates

in the History of Playing Cards

and Their Use in Divination

ca. 600 BC   The idea of randomizing with cards originates in
              divination rituals associated with the Cumaean sibyls.

1377   The 52-card deck is first mentioned and described in a
              manuscript written by the German monk, Johannes of
              Basel. With a few minor changes in the design of court
              cards and suit signs, the deck described by Johannes is
              nearly identical to what we find in modern American
              playing cards.

1442   The date assigned by scholars for the invention of Tarot
              cards, thought to be a product of Northern Italy. Claims
              by occultists of more ancient origins and occult
              applications are unsubstantiated by historical documents.

1448   The four card suits are divided into red and black
              components by French card manufacturers.

1540   In Europe fortune-telling using playing cards appears for
              the first time in a parlor game published by Francisco
              Marcoloni da Forlí of Venice, Italy.

1548   French cardmakers begin giving names and personalities
              to their court cards—an extremely useful idea in card
              reading.

1685	The first cards specifically designed for fortune-telling appear in London. This was a regular playing-card deck printed with occult symbolism and instruction for interpretation.
1765	The first written account of fortune-telling with cards is made by Casanova in his memoirs.
1770	Jean-Baptiste Alliette, a Frenchman who used the psuedonym Etteilla, published an elaborate system of card reading using a full Piquet deck, viz. an ordinary 52-card deck with all lower cards from Two to Six removed.
1778	The card calendar is mentioned for the first time in a pamphlet written in French and published in the city of Brussels.
1781	Antoine Court de Gébelin, a French scholar, publishes a book connecting Tarot cards with the ancient Egyptian Book of Thoth, the God of Magic. Prior to this publication, Tarot cards had no occult associations and were used only for playing a specific type of trump game.
1783	Etteilla (Jean-Baptiste Alliette) publishes *Cartonomancy, or the Art of Card Reading*... This gave rise to modern 'cartomancie,' and so to English 'cartomancy' as a term for fortune-telling with cards.
ca. 1850	Parlour fortune-telling becomes a popular diversion in England and France. Regular playing cards were used.
1939	A fifteenth-century hand painted deck of Egyptian playing cards is discovered at the Topkapi Sarayi Museum in Istanbul. The deck originally contained 52 cards. Curiously, the court cards have no images of people, only an inscription denoting their rank and suit.
2002	*The Picture Book of Ana Cortez* is published in connection with *The Playing Card Oracles: A Source Book for Divination*.

$\mathcal{M}$issing $\mathcal{P}$ieces
of the $\mathcal{P}$laying $\mathcal{C}$ard $\mathcal{P}$uzzle

$\mathcal{P}$LAYING CARD HISTORY IS COMPLICATED, very incomplete, and fascinating. Turns out there is a secret hidden in the playing card deck. Today that secret remains largely forgotten and only reveals itself in disconnected fragments, like pottery shards that are scattered about but obviously, at one time, had fit neatly together and made a complete object. In this case, enough pieces survive to reconstruct the object and yet in the end it's only a reconstruction, because many pieces remain missing. Nonetheless, by this process something lost for centuries can be recovered and seen again. What emerges is hardly the ordinary thing we've all examined and assume to be merely a collection of numbered markers used for playing games. In fact, it's a rather extraordinary thing designed to foresee events in time and, in effect, foretell the future.

My approach to this subject is by no means comprehensive. The history of playing cards and their development over centuries is a large subject that has already been documented by scholars far more capable than myself. Initially my interest in playing cards was more artistic than academic. In 1976 I began to re-draw the modern deck, focusing on the court figures, which impressed me as being too stylized to be really effective as images. Over the years I have re-drawn the entire deck top to bottom several times, and in the process become not only a frustrated artist, but something of a revisionist in my thinking. Researching the deck and its history, I soon realized there was more to playing cards than meets the eye. The tip-off is the exact correspondence of the 52-card deck to an ancient calendar. While largely ignored by scholars, the curious card calendar has been described *ad nauseam* by popular writers looking for interesting tidbits to liven up the Sunday supplement. But for some inexplicable reason, no one has tried to answer the obvious question: why put a calendar in a deck of cards? I think it is safe to say that whatever the answer, these associations with a calendar certainly hint at another application for playing cards beyond the scope of any known card game.

Unfortunately, no one knows who invented playing cards or when exactly this was done. The deck as we know it today descends from a European model, which is first described by the German monk Johannes of Basel in a Latin manuscript dated 1377. This manuscript clearly establishes the existence of playing cards in Europe by the third quarter of the fourteenth century. Johannes describes the deck as it was presented to him, mentioning the numbered pips and court cards with Kings as the thirteenth card in each of four suits. This was a deck of cards that resembles the deck we know today. Playing cards of some sort were known in China in the twelfth century but those cards were a different animal altogether, bearing little resemblance to the playing cards with which we are familiar. Modern American playing cards came directly from the English, whose model was provided by the French. Over centuries of use, certain changes have been made in our deck, primarily to accommodate game players. The widespread adoption of double-ended designs and card indexes are two worth mentioning. The Joker is an American innovation added in the late nineteenth century.[1] While certainly noteworthy, none of these additions are all that

---

[1] It is often thought the modern Joker derives from the Tarot Fool or Matto. Certainly a Joker suggests a fool and vice versa but, beyond that, there appears to be no connection. If a connection existed, we would expect to find some form of this character in early Italian playing cards that predate the Tarot by nearly seventy years. These decks had fifty-two cards with no extra card functioning as a Joker.

The Joker originated in the United States around 1870 and was first used in the game of Euchre. It was soon adopted for use in Poker and Rummy, where it served as a wild card. The Joker came to Europe with these games. "Since the Joker was invented at a time and place at which the Tarot pack was virtually unknown, we have to regard the resemblance between the Joker and the Fool of the Tarot pack as due to no more than pure coincidence." (*The Game of Tarot*, Michael Dummett, Duckworth, Ltd. London. 1980. pp. 7-8.)

important to our discussion. It's what has been removed from the deck that is important.

The practice of naming each court figure is an interesting idea found in early French decks. Some decks even provided slogans or mottoes for all the pip cards. These identifying names varied over time and by region but served a unique function. Once they had names, the cards took on character and were no longer simply numbers. In effect, they assumed a personality. Each had a story to tell, which could be read as in a book, a book of pictures.

When I first looked at playing cards as a child, I was fascinated by the court figures, or card people, as I called them. For me, these twelve cards represented people, and as such, they should have a name and a personality like a person. French cardmakers had the right idea. Unfortunately, all this was left behind when playing cards crossed the Channel from France to England. For whatever reason, English cardmakers chose not to name their cards, which they began producing in great numbers when the importation of playing cards was forbidden by royal decree in 1628. The English wholeheartedly adopted the suit signs along with the pip and court designs of French cards, but the idea of card personalities was nowhere to be found. What we are left with today is a deck ideally designed for gaming and little else. Basically, it is a collection of numbers, but maybe there is more in the numbers than we think.

The "Art of Numbers," or numerology, is an ancient form of divination that is credited to Pythagoras, a Greek mathematician of the sixth century B.C. The Pythagorean System concerns itself with the hidden meanings behind numbers, particularly the first nine numbers known as root numbers. Hidden number meanings can be found in much of the literature written in the Middle Ages and even in the architecture of some buildings, churches in particular, so it's not inconceivable that, following this tradition, hidden meanings were attached to the pip cards. These meanings may have been hidden in the sense that they weren't written on the actual cards, but the values attached to each number were never secret. Any interested party, then or now, can access this information and find a ready-made set of values for the pip cards 1 through 9. Numbers after 9—the so-called compound numbers—are seen as variations of the original nine root numbers.

Without a doubt, the first nine pip cards are identified with numbers, but what of the 10? Was the 10 in each suit always a numbered pip as it appears today? In the standard deck, numeral cards are identified by a field of pips or suit signs that correspond to their number value. In other words, a 10 of Hearts has ten Heart pips on its face, no other design. That's the way it's always been in the standard deck, with one notable exception. In the sixteenth century, both German and Swiss cardmakers represented the 10 in each suit not by a pip card with ten suit signs, but by a card showing a banner with a single suit sign. This created an unusual-looking card. Essentially, the 10 was given a design more in keeping with that of a court card than a numbered pip. What were these early cardmakers up to, if anything? Today, nearly four hundred years after its first appearance, the so-called Banner 10 can still be found in Swiss playing card decks, but the question remains.

At one point in his commentary on the curious new game of cards, Johannes of Basel describes the court figures in each suit as being a King and his attendant and a Queen and her attendant—presumably either a Lady-In-Waiting or a Lady of her chamber (*A History of Playing Cards*, Roger Tilley, Clarkson, Potter, Inc., New York, NY. 1973, p. 19). A regular deck with four court cards is unusual but not without precedent. Regular decks with four court cards were printed in Germany during the fifteenth century. One has to wonder how a fourth court card could have been added without increasing the number of cards in each suit to fourteen, which would do irreparable damage to the deck's calendar correspondences. Happily, there is another option suggested by numerology.

Given the opportunity, a numerologist would probably design our playing cards a little differently than what we find today in the modern deck. He certainly would not lump the pip cards 1 through 10 together. As we have seen, the 10 in each suit is a compound number, and, consequently, should be separated from the other nine pip cards, which represent root numbers. How better to separate the 10 than by changing its appearance? Hence, the Banner 10. If this is, in fact, the idea behind the banner design, then it is possible the 10 in other decks was redesigned as a fourth court card (the Queen's attendant) for the same reason. This presumes that numerology played an important role in determining how the playing card deck was perceived by some cardmakers back in the sixteenth century. Is there any evidence to corroborate such a claim for numerology? I think so.

In numerology, the odd numbers are often characterized as male numbers and the even numbers as female. For centuries, as the deck of playing cards slowly took on a definitive form in Europe, cardmakers followed this directive by putting the two male courts in male number positions, leaving the Queen as the twelfth card in each suit, a female position. The Lady of each suit would fit right into this male/female design as the 10, another female number. That gives us four courts in each thirteen-card suit—two male and two female all on appropriate male/female numbers. Could such an arrangement be coincidental? Maybe, but I doubt it. Taking card history and all this business about numbers into account, it's obvious the Lady is both a suitable and proper addition to the playing card court and, in our opinion, should therefore be reintroduced. Perhaps the most compelling argument is from the point of view of aesthetics. Adding a female court card in the 10 position of each suit creates a perfect symmetry of genders in an otherwise male-dominated court. This arrangement beautifully illustrates Pythagorian ideas about male and female numbers as well as the root numbers. It all fits and is pleasing to both the mind and the eye. "Make it so," as Picard would say. End of case.

Apart from numerology, there is another idea on cards and their numbers that deserves attention. In an age of computers, I suppose it was inevitable that someone would observe the essentially binary structure of playing cards (odd/even, red/black) and compare the deck to a medieval computer of some sort. Several authors have done just that but without developing the idea any further. If it's a computer, what on earth does it compute? No one seems to know, so the whole idea, while tantalizing, goes nowhere, like so many other ideas on this subject.

Suppose you're an investigator and you are given a case to solve. What sort of questions would you want answered? Surely you would need to know who was involved, for starters. You might also want to know where the event took place and when, things like that. Researching playing cards, I found all these important questions are left unanswered by historians writing during the Middle Ages. As a matter of fact, they seem to have been as much in the dark as we are today some six hundred years later. I dare say, there is probably nothing with such widespread cultural significance we know less about than the playing cards. For another point of view on the subject, I turned to the occult.

The many calendar associations found in the deck's structure suggested playing cards might have been used to forecast events over the course of a lunar year. From today's perspective, this would be considered occult. Modern occultism is truly a wilderness of tangled ideas piled one on top of another. There are scores of methods for forecasting events (numerology included), all of which fit into the general category known as divination. After looking over several books on this subject, I felt I was fast becoming lost in a briar patch of archaic beliefs. I needed help.

One day in an antique shop, lost in a pile of old magazines, I happened upon a book. It was minus its cover but the title page was intact: *The Cardboard Court*, by Dennis Holsey, 1943. At first, I thought it was a magazine, as there proved to be very little text. The pages mostly consisted of black and white photographs of European playing cards. I paid a small amount and took the book home. Several days passed before I looked at my new purchase carefully and discovered a lost piece of the playing card puzzle. On page twenty-one of Holsey's book, there was a photograph of a King of Clubs with his suit sign in the upper left and a collection of dots in the upper right. Of course, the dots were left unexplained. To me, the King of Clubs looked eighteenth century, but the dots were something I'd never seen before. With a bit of work—actually quite a bit—I found they represented one of sixteen figures (patterns of dots) used in geomancy, an ancient form of divination popular in Europe and many Islamic countries during the late Middle Ages and even earlier.

Right off, putting one geomantic figure on a particular card seemed like a mistake; after all, there are fifty-two cards in a deck, not sixteen. Exactly how this idea should connect with playing cards did not occur to me until sometime later.

In practice, geomantic figures are never simply assigned; they are computed. This is done by counting a number of randomized dots and determining whether they are odd or even. It is really very simple.

Certainly playing cards are readymade for these kinds of computations as the deck is neatly divided between odd and even numbers and red and black cards. The King of Clubs with a geomantic symbol on its face represented nothing short of an evolutionary leap in playing card design. Suddenly, the information available in a spread of cards increased dramatically. The uses of geomancy in playing card divination is discussed in the main text, but geomancy was only part of the equation. A deep strata of magical ideas underlies the composition of the deck itself. Before we try to resolve some of the perplexing questions surrounding the card calendar, I want to discuss one other idea.

Using games to model reality is a modern idea with applications in economics, mathematics, and a number of other sciences. It is also of interest in cartomancy or divination using a deck of cards.

Interactions between chance and natural laws can account for nearly everything taking place in the physical universe. To some extent, most games incorporate these two fundamental principles (chance and a set of rules). A game is defined by its rules in much the same way as the world of physical occurrences is defined by natural laws that behave with unvarying uniformity and make our world more or less predictable.

In other words, someone who jumps off a ten-story building will probably end up dead because of the force exerted by gravity, one of the rules of the game nature dictates. I say the person who jumps will *probably* end up dead because we don't know for sure. There is another principle at work, remember? The principle of chance. This makes our world more or less unpredictable. Suppose at exactly the right moment a truck drives by with a load of pillows and the person who jumps miraculously lands on this bed of pillows. What happens then? The laws of nature have been subverted for a brief moment and the person lives to jump another day. As is apparent, at least from this example, timing is all-important. The truck came by at just the right time. Good timing and bad timing are often manifestations of chance or Lady Luck, the popular characterization of this principle. Keep in mind, neither of these two principles reigns supreme. They constantly interact on every level from the subatomic on up.

In card games, chance is brought into play by shuffling the deck in order to produce a randomized series of cards. Each player in the game will then select a pattern of cards that is not random in the hope of producing a winning hand. For example, when playing poker, you might select three Kings and a pair of Aces, creating a full house. Obviously, without an interaction between chance and the rules of playing poker, there would be no game. With few exceptions, each and every adult card game played with the regular deck is an ordering, selecting, coherence-making process that transcends pure randomness by the directive of rules. Rules make sense of the gibberish produced by chance and give it meaning within the context of a particular game. Interestingly enough, many card games model the very processes involved in the creation of life itself (chance, rules, and selection). The possibilities for modeling or imitating fundamental principles found in nature hint at applications tucked into a deck of cards that far exceed anything seen in ordinary card games where the rules and objectives of play have no significance outside the prescribed parameter of a game.

Using a deck of cards to imitate the formative principles of the universe is an unusual concept for a game. Traditionally, card games are Zero-sum games. In other words, one player wins and everybody else usually loses. So who wins in a game that mimics the forces of nature? Can there even be a winner in such a game, and if not, then what's the point?

Unlike the Big Bang that created the universe billions of years ago, card games probably originated in the ninth century A.D. with nothing more imposing than a shuffle. As far as games are concerned, the idea of mixing up pieces of paper into a random assortment that can then be evenly distributed was the "Big Bang," which created in an instant the primal material for a thousand different games. We probably have the Chinese to thank, if that's the right word. Essentially, shuffling introduces an element of chance into card games, and, as chance is by definition unpredictable, the temptation to gamble with cards and "juice up the game" is nearly irresistible. In fact, playing cards are so closely associated with gambling it's often singled out as a defining characteristic of card-play in general. Europeans have been gambling with playing cards for over six hundred years, and yet a close look at the deck raises questions.

As a randomizing device, the 52-card deck has a rather complex structure for games of chance. In many cases, the simpler idea of randomizing numbers by casting dice would work just as well. So why the complexity of numbers, suits, and pictures in playing cards? This is where the deck gets really interesting, because for some reason its structure models an ancient calendar—suddenly, the concept of time is added to the mix.

The many numerical comparisons between the deck of playing cards and a calendar are quite remarkable. The fifty-two cards in a deck suggest the fifty-two weeks of the year. Having thirteen cards in each suit suggests the thirteen lunar months of the year and the thirteen weeks in each quarter. The four suits in a deck suggest the four seasons of the year. And finally, if we add up all the numbers in the deck counting Jacks as 11, Queens as 12, and Kings as 13, we get a total of 364. This number has created a good deal of controversy in modern times because we think of a year as being 365 days, not 364. Popular writers of the last century have proposed a number of remedies trying to put this little problem to bed, but none of their solutions are really satisfying. For instance, the idea of adding the Joker into the equation with a numerical value of 1 brings the total to 365 and seems to solve the problem for most everybody. But the Joker was nowhere in sight in the fourteenth century when the deck as we know it originated. So what were they thinking back then? We need to remember the Gregorian calendar we use today is calculated by using the sun, but in agricultural societies, farmers still determine their planting seasons by observing the moon, which has thirteen cycles over the course of a lunar year. For thousands of years, people have been interested in the moon primarily because of its profound effect upon the earth. Our seasons of planting and harvest, the tides used by fishermen, and even women's menstrual cycles all seem to be in step with the moon.

If we divide 13, the number of lunar revolutions per year, into 364, we get 28, an exact number of days for each cycle. But the number of days in each lunar cycle is not exact. They vary over the course of a lunar year, sometimes by as much as several days. So how can we have a lunar calendar when the deck dictates a twenty-eight day cycle, nothing more, nothing less? Perhaps there is another calendar.

Whoever created the deck of playing cards left no instruction manual for its use, so the only thing that can speak for their intentions is the deck itself. Because of this, it is important to leave the deck alone and not tamper with the evidence. The suggestion that we take the modern Joker, which to my knowledge has never been given a number value, and add it to the total so the deck will equal 365, is a good example of evidence tampering. Remember, without adding the Joker we get another number, 364, or 3 + 6 + 4, which totals 13. The number 13 is a key number in the organization of the deck, which has thirteen cards in each of four suits. Of course, it also figures into the lunar calendar, which has thirteen cycles. Additionally, the thirteen cards in each suit can be added together and the total is 91, or the number of days in a season. If we then divide 91 by 7, the number of days in a week, we again arrive at 13, the number of weeks in a season. We need to leave the deck alone and let it speak. The cards are telling us in a loud voice, "Pay heed, the number 13." In fact, it is the organizing number for the entire deck and its calendar.

In the late sixteenth century, Pope Gregory XIII convened a counsel to reform the Julian Calendar, which had been predominate in Western countries since the time of Julius Caesar. One proposal suggested replacing the Julian Calendar completely and adopting what was described as a Fixed Calendar. In this calendar the year consists of thirteen equal months of exactly twenty-eight days each. The months are all identical and each contains four weeks. After some deliberation, the idea was rejected, and would be of little interest today, except that the same calendar turns up in playing cards. We know the Fixed Calendar existed long before the time of Pope Gregory. In fact, it is a very old idea. The ancient Mayans living in Central America and parts of Mexico built the identical calendar correspondences into their temples at Chichen Itza and other locations.

The Fixed Calendar was never used in Europe, primarily because the number 13 is not easily divisible and proved cumbersome for simple calculations. There is also the superstition about the number 13. Despite all this, the Calendar fits perfectly into our deck of cards and probably dictated its design in the first place. It should be noted that in the Fixed Calendar under consideration by Pope Gregory, the 365th day of the solar year was not named or counted, but simply designated as a holiday. As mentioned, this calendar was never widely accepted. But the Muslim calendar is a Fixed Calendar, which has been used in many countries for centuries. This calendar has 360 Lunar months containing 10,631 days with an error of only one day every 2500 years. Of course, this probably didn't overly impress a Christian Pope. At any rate, the idea of incorporating a calendar into a deck of playing cards is ingenious both in its conception and application.

It wasn't until 1778, four hundred years after playing cards first appeared in Europe, that the deck's many calendar associations were mentioned in a pamphlet written in French and published in the city of Brussels. The pamphlet was later translated and circulated in England as a broadside under the title *The Perpetual Almanack, or, A Gentleman-Soldier's Prayer-Book*. As near as I can tell, this is the first written reference to the card calendar. It's been mentioned innumerable times since then, but never satisfactorily explained or put to use. Evidently, whoever created playing cards kept a secret. Today their secret is known and yet a mystery remains. Why put a calendar in a deck of cards? What purpose could it serve?

A deck of cards custom-made to accommodate a fixed yearly calendar is an unusual gaming device by anyone's definition; you might as well try playing a game with Fibonaccis numbers or magic squares. Although fascinating, none of these ideas are very useful in playing games, at least not the kinds of games normally associated with playing cards. There is one card game, however, in which a calendar would be extremely useful if not essential. Imagine a game where there are no winning cards, only combinations of cards that provide information of some kind. Conceivably, such a game could use a calendar to organize this information and make predictions for the coming year. In essence, the deck itself would function as an instrument of divination. If this was in fact the idea, then the popular perception of playing cards is misguided and has been for the past six hundred years.

Calendars written on papyrus and buried in royal tombs are among the earliest known publications. One in the British museum dates from the time of Ramses II (1290-1223 B.C.) and includes information on lucky and unlucky days as well as predictions on the fate of children born at certain times of the year. It seems the idea of using a calendar for prognostication developed early in Egyptian culture. Coincidentally, this is the same part of the world where playing cards are thought to have developed. If the truth be known, it may well turn out that the deck of cards first seen in Europe during the fourteenth century was originally designed for the ancient art of predicting the future by means of a calendar encoded with suits, numbers, and pictures.

By the seventeenth century, the term "playing cards" had become synonymous with the 52-card deck because in Europe it was used to play games, pure and simple (*chartae lusoriae, cartes à jouer, Spielkarten, carte da giuoco*, etc.). This association can be seen from the very beginning, when Johannes of Basel in 1377 speaks not of a deck of cards, but of a game of cards, which suggests that cards were used to play a particular type of game. Unfortunately, Johannes does not describe the game except to say it was played in "one way or another." That these early games involved gambling is evident from a number of manuscripts dating to the late Middle Ages, which condemn both playing cards and dice for their uses in gambling.

Gambling games in their simplest form are won or lost largely by chance, and involve few skills beyond a most rudimentary knowledge of the game. Dice were designed for these kinds of games, which have been played in Europe since Roman times and enjoyed great popularity in the fourteenth century. It's a safe bet no one appreciated the versatility of playing cards initially, but their obvious randomizing capabilities undoubtedly impressed Europeans.

It almost seems like playing cards were made for games of chance, except that, unlike dice, which produce no more information than what can be deduced from a limited series of numbers, a deck of fifty-two cards, equally divided into four suits of thirteen cards each, is a large canvas that can generate a wealth of information. This is not always useful in games of chance, which usually thrive on simplicity. In any card game, too much information can inhibit play and confuse the game, so the possibilities of the 52-card deck are necessarily limited in popular games. Over the years, card games have become more sophisticated, and yet to date, no popular game uses the full potential of the 52-card deck. On the other hand, in cartomancy, or divination with cards, every feature of the playing card deck is essential. Popular games have arbitrary rules that decide what combination of cards wins the game. By contrast, there is no such thing as a winning hand in cartomancy. Quite literally, nothing can be safely ignored, and everything counts, at least potentially. As a general rule, in divination of any kind, the more information you can muster, the better. The conceptual difference between cartomancy and all other card games is striking.

Among other things, the unique calendar structure of the 52-card deck organizes information into fifty-two weeks, covering a year's time. Such a concept could only be useful in divination. This tells us something about the people who created our playing cards in the fourteenth century. That they had magic in mind is apparent from the deck itself. It is really the only document we have that can speak across centuries and provide insight into what these people might have been thinking.

Incidentally, historians think that the Tarot was created in northern Italy around 1440, nearly seventy years after regular playing cards were first seen in Europe. Tarot was originally designed to play trump card games like *Tarocchi*, and has no history of occult applications until the late eighteenth century (*The Game of Tarot*, Michael Dummett, Duckworth, London, 1980).[2]

For some reason, Tarot cards, which were originally created for card games, have evolved into a fortune-telling deck. On the other hand, playing cards, with their built-in calendar designed for divination, are used to play a variety of popular games, none of which involve divination. Ahh, the irony of it all!

---

[2] The idea that Tarot goes back to ancient Egypt originated with Antoine Court de Gébelin in 1781 and has been promoted by occultists ever since. There is no historical evidence to substantiate these claims.

The Little Book of Secrets

WHY IS THERE SO LITTLE HISTORICAL INFORMATION on the origin of European playing cards? This question has puzzled nearly everyone who has studied the subject.

We need to remember that in Europe during the fourteenth century the Catholic Church aggressively persecuted people for beliefs and practices it opposed. From the Church's point of view, the many gambling applications found in a deck of cards were the very stuff of hell-fire and damnation, so if a person created such a thing, they certainly wouldn't go around bragging about it, and apparently nobody did. That's one possible explanation for the lack of information on the subject, if we assume playing cards originated in Europe. There is yet another explanation that is not nearly so speculative.

History would have us believe that playing cards simply materialized like faerie gold one bright summer's day sometime in the late fourteenth century. Their appearance was totally unanticipated. Just the concept of using pieces of paper as a randomizing device was a newfangled idea in Europe at the time. It is doubtful many people knew how sophisticated the idea really was; six hundred years later most of us still don't have a clue.

Seems nobody had seen or heard of anything like playing cards until they were confronted by a complete deck all spread out on a table, ready for play. Stranger things have happened, but it is unlikely something so new and complex could be created overnight. When you think about it, the sudden appearance of playing cards makes little sense unless the 52-card deck only came to Europe after developing somewhere else.

Some scholars suggest the four-suited Chinese Money Pack as the prototype, even though it comes up short of fifty-two cards in any of its several variations. Additionally, there are no court cards in the Money Pack that we recognize. The same can be said of its suit signs, which would have been unintelligible to Europeans of the late Middle Ages. In the last analysis, the Money Pack is a difficult match for the playing cards first introduced into Europe.

Another more probable hypothesis points to the Islamic world. If playing cards first arrived in Europe in 1377 or thereabouts, they most likely came from a source close to Europeans. This would have to be an Islamic country, as Europe at that time had no direct contact with any other part of the world. There was no trade with either India or China, so anything from these countries had to pass through an encircling belt of Muslim states to reach Europe during the fourteenth century. After his travels in Asia, Marco Polo (1254–1324?) could have introduced Chinese playing cards to Venice, but there is no indication that he did.

Although cards probably originated in China as a means of gambling, many scholars believe the 52-card deck is a product of Islamic design. Several Medieval Islamic cards (actually fragments of cards) have been identified and dated to the thirteenth century by reliable sources. The most complete example of Medieval Islamic playing cards can be found in Istanbul at the Topkapi Sarayi Museum. This beautiful hand-painted deck originally contained fifty-two cards (forty-eight survive) and consisted of four suits—Swords, Polo Sticks, Cups, and Coins, each composed of ten numeral cards and three court cards. It is the oldest surviving deck of Islamic design and bears an uncanny resemblance to the 52-card deck we use today, except that there are no figures drawn on any of the twelve court cards, only an inscription in Arabic giving their rank and suit.

The absence of images depicting the human form is a characteristic feature of Islamic religious art. For example, there are no surviving medieval manuscripts of the Koran embellished with drawings of people. Artists were limited to geometric and floral designs. By contrast, images of people abound in Islamic secular manuscripts, so why the reluctance to include these images on playing cards? What could be more secular than a deck of cards? Surely, whoever designed the deck was aware of the distinction between secular and religious Islamic art, and the risks they were taking by stylistically associating their creation with the latter. In medieval times, such an association could be construed as blasphemous and a threat to the established traditions of Islam. The *ulama*, who acted as the guardians of tradition and became a kind of clergy with police powers, considered blasphemy to be deserving of the most severe punishment—death by the sword, or beheading.

In the late Middle Ages, traditional Islamic beliefs were threatened not only by a resurgence of Sufi mysticism, but other more radical ideas as well. Members of the Hurufi sect, for example, gained attention toward the end of the fourteenth century by claiming to possess secret knowledge that enabled them to calculate numerical values found in verses of the Koran and predict the future. Divination in any form is explicitly forbidden in the later suras of the Koran itself, but obviously such prohibitions were ignored by Ismaili groups like the Hurufi, who were persecuted relentlessly. One of their more prominent members, the Turkish poet Nesimi, was tortured and killed in 1417.

Fear of persecution may explain why so little is known about the creators of Islamic playing cards. Unconventional ideas always arouse suspicion in a repressive society. Silence does not. Knowing this, a wise man would keep his eyes open and his mouth shut. Evidently, that's exactly what the cardmakers responsible for the 52-card deck decided to do. Virtually nothing is known about these people. Nonetheless, we are left with a deck of medieval Islamic playing cards discovered in 1939 on display at the Topkapi Sarayi museum in Istanbul. As mentioned, the deck has no images of the human form on any of its twelve court cards, which at first glance raises more questions than it answers. Of course, the most interesting thing about the Topkapi Sarayi deck is its composition. Having fifty-two cards equally divided into four suits of thirteen cards each created a calendar, which suggests that the deck may have been designed for divination. This undoubtedly tells us something about its maker but the more one tries to understand their thinking, the less sense it makes. One has to wonder how randomizing a collection of pasteboard markers that corresponded to a calendar could reveal anything of importance. What was it they saw that we fail to see six hundred years later?

Few people realize that throughout the Middle East, Europe, and Asia, ancient civilizations used randomizing devices to reveal the will of their gods. According to Proverbs, 16:30, "the lot is cast ... but the whole disclosing thereof is of the Lord." In other words, long before the advent of Islam, Hebrews who lived during the time of the Old Testament believed that chance instruments were moved by the hand of God, and could be read as an expression of His will. From this belief it was a small step to believing that one could determine God's will by randomizing with cards.

Dice had been in existence for thousands of years by the time playing cards first developed in China during the T'ang dynasty (618–906 A.D.). This was a major innovation in the art of randomizing, that redefined Chinese gambling games, giving them a degree of complexity impossible to achieve with the limitations imposed on a six-sided cubicle die. The idea quickly spread beyond the borders of China.

Islamic cards began their journey westward when *ganjifa* decks from Muslim communities in India trickled into Iran and became the progenitor for a 96-card Persian deck that substituted rectangular-shaped cards for the traditional circular cards found in India. The Persian deck eventually found its way to Egypt, where a remarkable transformation occurred sometime in the first half of the fourteenth century.

Medieval Persian cards were hand-painted on materials such as ivory, wood and cotton fiber, and leather. Consequently, the cards could be bulky and difficult to handle. In addition, suitmarks varied from deck to deck, as did the images. For anyone unfamiliar with the peculiar iconography of Persian cards, the prospect of playing a game with such an unwieldy deck must have been daunting, to say the least. All things considered, it's not surprising that Egyptian cardmakers created an entirely new Islamic deck. The new deck consisted of fifty-two pasteboard cards equally divided into four suits of thirteen cards each. Rather than an assortment of different images, the first ten cards of each suit were all illustrated similarly with simple geometric shapes corresponding to the suit and number value of each card. Compared to Persian cards, the 52-card deck was a marvel of simplicity. Ironically, the ideas behind the deck's design were anything but simple.

Just for a moment, try conceptualizing the 52-card deck as a *book* of cards with fifty-two unbound pages. Not that playing cards were ever referred to in these terms, but the concept may have influenced Islamic cardmakers nonetheless. Before we can understand their thinking, we need to break free of the perception that playing cards were designed for popular games.

Since time immemorial, men have sought to foresee the future. In most cases, divination consisted of relatively simple procedures, as in the binary calculations of odd and even used in geomancy. Playing cards have similar binary components and came to Europe from the Arab world at about the same time, but Islamic cards were seen as a different animal. As far as anyone knew, playing cards were for playing games, nothing more. Divination using cards was a more complex idea unimagined by Europeans until the sixteenth century.

The word 'cartomancy' as a term for fortune-telling with cards was first used by a Frenchman who called himself *Etteilla* (Jean Baptiste Alliette), in a book entitled *Cartonomancy, or, the Art of Card-Reading...*, published in 1783. This is the earliest occurrence of the word, which gave rise to modern 'cartomancie,' and so to English 'cartomancy' as a term for card reading. Although the word originated in the eighteenth century, the concept has its roots in antiquity.

It seems like telling fortunes with cards began in Europe with Francesco Marcolino da Forlí, who wrote a book on the subject, published in Venice in 1540. Turns out Marcolino's book was not a treatise on divination so much as a booklet with instructions on playing a parlor game. His fortune-telling game required an Italian-suited regular deck shortened to thirty-six cards. In this particular game, reading the booklet was more important than reading the cards, which were given no individual meaning beyond that of an auxiliary randomizing mechanism similar to dice. As we shall see shortly, divination with cards predates Renaissance parlor games, which anticipate the fortune-telling games contrived by Victorian publishers in the nineteenth century but provide little insight into the magical ideas of an earlier time.

In truth, it's difficult to imagine divination with cards much before the invention of paper in the eighth century A.D. And yet, as previously mentioned, cards can be made of other materials. Interestingly enough,

Roman commentaries on the oracles of ancient Cumae provide some evidence that the idea of randomizing with cards first developed in divination and only later came to be used for playing games.

The sibylline books were a collection of oracle verses attributed to an order of seers known as sibyls, who set up shop in Cumae, on the Bay of Naples, around 600 B.C. Prophecies written in verse probably required the assistance of attending priests to transcribe the sibyls' admonitions and rewrite them in verse on sheets of papyrus or thin sheets of wood called leaves (leaves of a book?). In Book III of *The Aeneid* by Virgil (70 B.C.–19 B.C.) we are told that the leaves were shuffled and chosen at random by petitioners seeking divine guidance. If this was true, then cartomancy dates back to the Cumaean sibyls. The idea would remain entombed in Virgil's *Aeneid* for centuries before being rediscovered and given new life by a small community of Arab intellectuals.

During the Middle Ages, fascination with classic Greek and Roman literature led to an intellectual awakening in the Muslim world unequaled in Europe before the Italian Renaissance. In fact, as early as the ninth century, it's likely that Arab scholars first learned of the sibyls from translating the poetic works of Ovid and Virgil.

Knowledge of the sibyls might have cast an entirely different light on the potential of Persian playing cards, which came to Egypt as trade expanded during the thirteenth and fourteenth centuries. Changing popular perceptions was no less of a challenge back then than it is today, and yet, as divination with cards was unknown at the time, something alerted Arab cardmakers to other possibilities for playing cards besides their obvious applications in popular games. That something may well have been the sibylline oracles. What better vessel for randomizing a collection of oracles than a collection of pasteboard cards? Of course, up to this point it's all speculation, but there can be little doubt that the medieval Islamic playing cards preserved in Istanbul were designed for some sort of divination. Anyone who examines the cards carefully can see that they correspond to a calendar. What's more, the twelve court cards have no images of people, in keeping with Islamic traditions prohibiting inclusion of such images in religious manuscripts. This suggests that the card calendar was somehow a sacred calendar. It's a safe bet none of these things were accidental, so what are the implications? Let's connect the dots: 1) We know that ancient civilizations used randomizing to determine the will of their god or gods. Cards are a randomizing device. 2) Foreseeing the future involves the concept of time. A calendar measures time. 3) It's been said that the future is for God to know and men to imagine. Presumably, any book revealing things only God can know would be considered sacred, even a book of cards. Who could guess that such an unimposing little book with just fifty-two pages told stories not only of the past, but stories of the future as well? If this approximates the thinking of Arab cardmakers, then the 52-card Islamic deck was nothing less than a book of divine revelations. Essentially, an old belief had been revitalized by an extraordinary new idea. That leaves us with the tantalizing question of how the idea worked in reality.

Devout Muslims who farmed their land undoubtedly prayed to Allah, asking for His blessing on a harvest to be gathered in the fall. Would their prayers be answered? God knows, the summer months might bring an infestation of locusts, or a killing drought. Should they plant a crop or leave their fields fallow? For questions of this sort, the 52-card deck became a kind of prayer book unlike any other, in that it gave petitioners an idea of what they could expect from God in the future through the genius of a built-in calendar. For example, a farmer worried about summer drought might shuffle the deck and interpret whatever cards corresponded to that time of year. In this respect, unlike the Koran, which represents the unadulterated word of God as revealed to His prophet Muhammad, the deck of fifty-two cards could be interpreted as revealing the will of God, not through the words of a prophet but in a rubric written by chance. Needless to say, any such ideas completely eluded Europeans of the fourteenth century, who saw another more obvious use for cards and quickly put the 52-card deck to work as a randomizing device for games of chance. It's unlikely that people living in Muslim countries were any more enlightened than their European counterparts. In all probability, only a select few had knowledge of the occult ideas built into the 52-card deck. For everyone else, the deck was perceived quite differently.

Before the invention of wood-block printing in the fifteenth century, cards were hand-painted and difficult to reproduce. As a result, card-play first appeared among the wealthy classes. Scholars have found just three references to Islamic cards in the literature composed by Muslims during medieval times. The most interesting is a passage found in the *Annals* written by Ibn Taghri-Biri in which mention is made of a large sum being won in a game of cards by the Sultan al-Malik. This occurred around 1400 A.D. and confirms that gambling with cards was known in Muslim countries not long after playing cards first appeared in Europe.

Even though gambling is forbidden by the Koran, it seems to have attracted many Muslims. As might be expected, Europeans ignored similar prohibitions by the Catholic Church. Gamblers will bet money on practically anything, but since the fourteenth century, their weapon of choice has been playing cards. Indeed, for many it's hard to imagine what else cards are good for besides gambling. Had people known that the 52-card deck was an exact model of a fixed lunar calendar, their perception of playing cards might have been very different, especially people living in the fourteenth century. Back then, anyone who modeled or imitated something could be accused of practicing magic.

Imitative magic (sometimes known as Sympathetic Magic) dates back to ancient times and was used during the Middle Ages primarily for the creation of charms and magic spells. Basically, it was thought that by imitating something, one could control it magically. The benefits of exercising one's will over someone or some thing are obvious, but constructing charms and spells for such a purpose seems fanciful at best. Sympathetic magic was also used to imitate things like the outcome of a battle or the prospects for a successful voyage. The idea of imitating a future event to gain some insight into its outcome is far more sophisticated. Even today, computer-generated models that imitate weather patterns or economic activity are used in forecasting. Looking at playing cards from a magical perspective, the randomizing of cards that occurs in shuffling could be seen as imitating the fluctuations of good and bad fortune over a year's time, as measured by the card calendar. In the Middle Ages, many Europeans thought in magical terms, but evidently no one thought of playing cards as being magical, which was probably a good thing given the mindset of the Catholic Church. Had the Church known of the secrets that lay buried in the 52-

card deck, anyone caught playing a game of cards could have been accused of practicing magic and possibly burned at the stake. But the Church had no clue.

Europeans learned of the card calendar in 1778, centuries after playing cards first appeared in Europe. Apparently, the Islamic cardmakers who designed our playing cards buried their secret in their creation and never told another living soul, certainly not a soul living in Europe. Who were these mysterious cardmakers anyway? No one knows. Unfortunately, playing card history is very incomplete, but taking into account the little we do know, it seems likely that the 52-card deck was designed by members of a secret order of some kind. In the Arab world of the fourteenth century, Islam and its institutions, much like the Catholic Church in Europe, claimed exclusive rights to all things magical, so anyone who infringed on their territory was put at risk. Obviously, in a repressive religious culture, no one with an ounce of sense took credit for anything that might be in opposition to sacred teachings. Because of this, what we are left with today is a near-total void of historical information on the creators of playing cards. The same can be said for the kinds of games they had in mind. Nothing is known.

Many scholars think that playing cards first came from a Muslim country through Venice, which was a major port of entry into Europe during the Middle ages. If this is true, then sailors undoubtedly were involved and quite possibly introduced the 52-card deck to Europeans. Of course, whoever was responsible said nothing about a calendar or any magical applications, probably out of ignorance.

When history has little to say on a given subject, it provides an opportunity for the storyteller. Some of my first stories were inspired by playing cards. Several of these stories are included in the main text. *The Little Book of Secrets*, which follows, tries to assemble what is known about the origin of playing cards and make some sense of it. This was difficult. The story makes little sense from the get-go. But whoever said history makes perfect sense? In reality, history, or what passes for history, becomes accessible to us only by way of the imagination. There is a logic apart from common sense found in the imagination, and it is this logic that inspired *The Little Book of Secrets* as surely as it inspired the history it portrays.

The Little Book of Secrets: A Story

*I*MAGINE THAT ONCE UPON A TIME, there existed an Islamic Brotherhood whose magical practices violated not only the teachings of the Koran, but Christian doctrine as well. Imagine also that the Brotherhood had created an instrument of magic, which they believed allowed them to see into the future. Bragging about their accomplishment would have been extremely unwise. More importantly, the Vows of Silence taken by all initiates of such an Order prohibited them from ever revealing their secrets to anyone, even if they had wanted to for whatever reason.

So time passed, and, as might be expected, the Brothers grew old and began to die, until finally only one Brother remained. Now, Brother Kalid Abu Alisomb lived much longer than the others, and the older he got, the more he feared Death. He had no fear of dying itself. Alisomb embraced the idea of being done with life, and in fact longed for the day. He feared Death because as there were no other surviving Brothers, when he died he knew the Brotherhood's secret would die with him. This troubled him greatly. Of course, he could find a young disciple, tell him the secret, and be done with it, but that would involve breaking his Vow of Silence, which he could never do. It seemed like an unsolvable problem, so Alisomb focused his attention on more immediate concerns. Being the last surviving Brother created any number of problems, not the least of which was arranging for his own burial in the monastery churchyard. Who could be trusted to bury him properly? By his calculation, the right person lived in or near a little fishing village not far from the monastery. Once he identified this person, Alisomb must face to the West and Death would come quickly. He further calculated the appointed time of his death as being the third week in June, under a sign of Acquisito, which was rather an odd sign, as Acquisito means comprehending or perceiving, concepts not normally associated with death. God in His wisdom left some things unexplained.

For even an ascetic monk, Alisomb lived modestly, with few resources he could depend on besides his garden, which had gone untended in recent months, becoming little more than a patch of weeds. Alisomb ate the last of his parsnips and peppers, along with several radishes, and began his fast in the seventh hour on the first day of the third week in June. From that point on, he planned to stay awake and eat nothing more for the rest of his life. After an hour of meditation, he bathed and dressed in clean linen, then walked three miles to reach the village where he believed Death awaited him.

The villagers feared the old man dressed in mourning clothes, especially as Alisomb appeared at the stroke of noon and stood with his eyes closed and arms crossed as if he had just been delivered up from the dead.

Everyone could see that he cast no shadow and wore white linen wrapped in the fashion of a shroud, and yet Alisomb lacked the pallor of a corpse. Nor did he have the transparency required of a ghost. Furthermore, the departed were known to be nocturnal by nature and usually avoided walking around in broad daylight. What manner of spirit would be so bold? The speculation created a panic.

Needless to say, things were not nearly as bad as they seemed. Anyone could see that with the sun directly overhead, few shadows were visible anywhere in the village. Even more telling, Alisomb had darkened skin from prolonged exposure to the sun. Now surely even the old wives, who rarely agreed on anything, would all agree that a spirit condemned to walk the village by day, and slowly burn in the sun, was extremely unusual, if not one of a kind. In reality, despite his odd choice of attire, Alisomb looked very much like any other toothless old man in that part of the world, but for some reason, reality impressed no one. Not only did the villagers see very little, none of them understood what they saw. And anyway, who had time to think clearly? In a matter of moments, every man, woman, and child in the village had fled to the safety of their houses.

Left to himself, Alisomb constructed a shelter of palm leaves and set up camp within a stone's throw of the sea, which flanked the village to the west and south. In the village, nothing stirred in any direction. Immersed in stillness, Alisomb was tempted to sleep, but feared that if he slept, he might sleep forever and never rest in peace. Rather than risk even so much as forty winks, he focused all his attention one last time on the problem of preserving the Brotherhood's secrets, which had been encoded and given to each Brother in the form of a little book. Try as he might, no solution had ever occurred to him, short of breaking his Vow of Silence, which he could never do. What, then, could he do? Every day, Alisomb prayed for an answer, and every day, Allah answered with silence. Evidently, God observed the same Vows as the Brotherhood. It occurred to Alisomb that just possibly, the Brothers' practice of using their Little Book to divine the future angered not only the many disciples of Muhammad, but Allah as well, and Allah had no interest in helping either him or the Brotherhood. Alisomb put aside these troublesome thoughts. It was enough for him to know that some things were best left unresolved, and he must accept God's indifference to his prayers, if that's what it was, or live without God, which was unthinkable.

No doubt, finding someone in the village to prepare a grave and bury his remains would be relatively simple. But days passed, and with each passing day it became more apparent that what appeared to be simple was in fact impossible. Each day Alisomb walked every foot of the village, knocked on every door, and found not one person who would talk with him. From the moment he first set foot in the village, people took shelter in their shanties, barricaded their doors, and hid in closets and under beds. Still, Alisomb persisted, and circled endlessly around the village, reciting verses from the Koran, and gave the villagers no rest. In the history of the village, no one could recall a haunting of such extraordinary proportions. Of course, given half a chance, Alisomb could have easily explained his behavior.

Unlike most men who live with no knowledge of their death, Alisomb knew when he would die—not an exact time but an approximate time—which was written in the Little Book and interpreted by him as being the third week in July of that year. Knowing only this much, he dare not sleep over the course of those seven days. Should Alisomb die in his sleep, the Brothers believed he might lose sight of the next world and wander the Earth forever. Sadly, although every Brother accepted this idea, and did everything in his power to stay awake, many died with their eyes closed and were buried as lost souls. All of this could easily be explained if anyone asked.

No one in the village understood how a man as old as Alisomb could live so long and not have to eat or sleep unless he was dead, which would explain his wearing a shroud. I mean, who would dress in a shroud if they weren't dead? Only in this case, no one rested in peace. At all hours Alisomb knocked on doors and chanted at the top of his voice, disturbing the peace of everyone in the village. Perhaps it was only some poor peddler who failed to realize he was dead and went door to door reliving the routine of his life. One thing for sure, listening to a dead man pitch his wares was too much to ask.

When Alisomb continued to march around their streets, the villagers became more aggressive. Some emptied their chamber pots and slop buckets the moment he passed, covering him in filth. Other times, young children threw stones and taunted him with sticks. Alisomb put up with all these things until an old fishwife swore to disembowel him if he knocked on her door one more time. At that point, Alisomb knew something must be done, but what should he do? Surely God had other plans for him. And so it was that the last Brother spent his last miserable day a mile down the coast, where he sat in utter solitude and cursed his fate with every breath he took until a fishing boat sailed into view. Just the thought of a fish prepared with skill and served for Sunday supper changed everything.

Instinctively, Alisomb raised both arms and recited a long benediction customarily said by the Brothers each day before breaking their fast. The boat continued on its northerly course until it seemed a breath of wind rose up and carried Alisomb's voice well out to sea. Within minutes, as if hearing the old man from half a mile away, the fisherman trimmed his sail, then tacked about and headed directly for shore. At that moment, Alisomb realized the boat he summoned now sailed from a point due west, the direction given by the Little Book and associated with his death. Alisomb fell to his knees and praised Allah with what must be his last breath; then he waited. But nothing happened, except that his mouth felt dry and his stomach kept reminding him that it was time to eat. At last, Alisomb climbed painfully to his feet and marvelled at the wisdom of God. He believed everything happened for a reason. Such a belief left little room for chance and led Alisomb to think that the fisherman must have been sent by God in answer to his many prayers on behalf of the Brotherhood.

The fisherman greeted him like a long-lost friend, and after a brief conversation, Alisomb learned he fished these waters with regularity and knew every village. Mostly, the man talked about his children, and, without mentioning any daughters, he boasted of his twenty-three sons, the oldest of which was just seventeen years. As far as the fisherman knew, this was a world record, and more sons were on the way. Apparently, he planned to provide enough men for an entire fleet of fishing boats bearing his name, and for that noble purpose, the fisherman befriended nearly every woman he met up and down the coast of the Red Sea. All in all, not exactly the kind of man Alisomb expected, but a perfect man for the task at hand. After hearing the fisherman talk for only a few minutes, Alisomb understood the logic that must have been in God's mind when He chose the fisherman as the one man more qualified than any other to save the Brotherhood's secrets from extinction. The plan was simple. Unlike all his brothers before him, Alisomb would not be buried with the Brotherhood's Little Book of Secrets held in his lifeless hand for all eternity. Instead, he gave the last copy of the Little Book to the fisherman.

The Book consisted of fifty-two unbound pages encrypted with symbols and looked very strange to the fisherman, but he was told that the Book could be used to play a variety of simple games anyone might understand, even a child. With that said and nothing more, Alisomb blessed the fisherman and returned home with a fine fish to cook for supper.

Death took its time and years passed. One day, while visiting the same village, Alisomb came upon some sailors from across the sea. The men were busy drinking wine and gambling, and took no notice of the withered figure who watched them. Finally, one sailor addressed Alisomb.

"You have jinxed my cards, old man," he said in an angry voice, and shook his fist. The sailor had lost all his money playing at cards while Alisomb watched transfixed, like he had never before seen anybody play a game of cards. "You are a jinx," the sailor repeated, continuing to shake his fist.

"Gambling is forbidden by the Koran," Alisomb replied matter-of-factly, then walked slowly away.

"What game would you have us play, old man?" asked another sailor.

"No other game," Alisomb answered, and smiled a big smile all the way home.

That night, the last surviving Brother greeted Death with his eyes wide open and the same curious smile still touching his lips. No doubt he saw the future.

OF COURSE, THIS IS JUST A STORY, but for all we know about the origin of playing cards, it could well be a true story. Imagine that.

Fire, Air, Water, and Earth

---

*T*HE CONCEPT OF THE FOUR ELEMENTS, which was first worked out by ancient Greek philosophers, reigned unchallenged well into the seventeenth century and would have been widely known when playing cards first appeared in Europe. The idea found application in Alchemy and held that all things material divided into four simple elements of Earth, Air, Fire, and Water, each of which exhibited discernable characteristics. This proved to be a useful construct for playing card divination. Almost from the very beginning, French cardmakers had provided names and personalities for the court figures[3]. This same approach could now be applied to the card suits themselves by identifying them with a particular element, essentially giving each suit a personality. There is no historical evidence indicating this was ever done in the fourteenth century, but then there is nothing to say it wasn't. The only evidence we have is found in the playing card deck itself, which easily accommodates the idea of connecting four elements to four suits. But which elements belong to which suits? The general consensus is with the suit of Cups or Hearts, which nearly everyone agrees should be associated with Water. As for the rest, opinions are all over the map. True enough, some associations seem better made than others, but in the last analysis it is the concept that matters most.

---

[3] Actually, the idea of naming the court cards first appeared at the end of the sixteenth century and never took hold outside of France. French cardmakers did divide the four card suits into red and black components. These red and black silhouettes first appeared about 1480 and are now an international design popular all over the world.

Fortune-Telling

*I*T'S PROBABLY HARD TO BELIEVE, but, in America, divination with cards was often done using regular playing cards up until rather recently, perhaps the last forty years or so. Tarot cards were hard to come by in this country before the early 1960s. Today, they are literally ubiquitous and have largely replaced playing cards for purposes of divination.

During Victorian times, divination with regular cards was quite popular and fit into a broad category of games designed primarily for entertainment. John Lenthall, an English stationer, offered an item to the public that he described in his catalogue as "Fortune-Telling Cards Pleasantly Unfolding the Good and Bad Luck Attending Human Life— Directions Included." Apparently these cards were made available for several decades during the reign of Charles II (1660–1685). These are the earliest known fortune-telling cards and had the suit signs and composition of a regular playing-card deck, but were encrypted with a bewildering array of other symbols. Those who have seen Lenthall's fortune-telling cards describe them as a specialty pack, not simply a regular deck of playing cards with directions for fortune-telling. There must have been a market for such things, because in 1703 we find a newspaper advertisement promoting "Diverting and Innocent Fortune-telling Cards," offered by H. Newman in Little Britain. A few years later, in 1705, there is another advertisement for fortune-telling cards at one shilling a pack offered for sale by a Mr. Fullowood at the Knave of Clubs in Paternoster Row. Obviously, fortune-telling with cards was popular in London nearly one hundred years before Court de Gébelin refashioned the Tarot into an engine of the occult in France. Oddly enough, the famous rogue and womanizer Giacomo Casanova provides the first written account of fortune-telling with cards in his memoirs. The entry is dated 1765 and involved regular playing cards, which were read by a young Russian woman who became Casanova's mistress for a time during his sojourn in Russia. Apparently, the worldly Casanova was unfamiliar with card reading before being introduced to the practice by this woman.

The Victorians turned fortune-telling into a game using regular playing cards in the mid-nineteenth century. For the most part, these rather simplistic games with cards were created for titillation and amusement in the parlor. Essentially, Victorian publishers reduced the idea to its lowest common denominator, that of cheap entertainment, and marketed their products for mass consumption. When the art of card reading became little more than a popular diversion, people with a real interest in the subject turned away from fortune-telling with regular cards and took up the Tarot. Tarot cards have dominated the scene ever since.

Card Personalities

*I*N OUR SPECIALLY DESIGNED DECK, we have followed the French tradition of naming court cards. La Hire, as the Jack of Hearts, and Lancelot, as the Jack of Clubs, have served in the French playing-card deck for centuries and are included in *The Picture Book of Ana Cortez*. All other court figures are unique to our deck. Creating our own card personalities was done for a number of reasons. First of all, we were not interested in simply re-creating a French deck. Furthermore, the names found in French decks vary over time and by region. So which do you choose?

We are indebted to the French in many ways, but numerology and the concept of the four elements were important factors in our thinking. There is scant evidence to suggest French cardmakers had any of this in mind when they named their court figures. It is probably happenstance that La Hire and Lancelot fit so nicely into the medieval ideas about elements associated with their respective suits. None of the other card personalities found in French decks fit nearly as well. This necessitated creating our own card personalities. Each court figure in our deck is characterized by the Element of its suit and its position in the playing-card court. For example, a King is given qualities in keeping with his high position, whereas a Jack is usually a less mature personality. In all cases, the character traits of the card in question are determined in large part by the qualities associated with the Element of that suit.

The pip cards are clearly identified with numbers, so numerology played a major role in characterizing these cards. Additionally, when appropriate, we took names from old card games where specific cards were given a name. For instance, the 9 of Diamonds was identified with the legendary Pope Joan in the game of Pope and would have made an interesting addition to our pack except that the 9 of each suit is a male number and seemed inappropriate as a female, even if she is the Pope. The 5 of Diamonds as The Peddlers Ace from the old game of Sixpence and the 3 of Diamonds as The Necklace from the game of Fetch were better suited and became part of our deck. The idea of using the Winds to give each suit a direction and specific energy originated in Ma Jong. Obviously, we looked far and wide for appropriate images to express each card's personality and be consistent with the various sets of correspondences we are using for the purposes of divination.

The court cards were no less of a challenge. Let me provide just one example: the Queen of Spades. French cardmakers often name their court cards after biblical characters. Additionally, names were taken from French history and Greek mythology. In the case of the Queen of Spades, we find all of these and then some. Pallas Athena, the Greek Goddess of Wisdom, La Pucelle, or Joan of Arc, and Betsabe (Bathsheba) all found a place in the French deck as the Queen of Spades during the fifteenth century.

And on it goes from there. I guess, like naming a child, it's pretty much a matter of personal preference.

In the popular imagination, the Queen of Spades has acquired rather dark nuances in modern times, which find expression in her role as a penalty card in such games as Black Maria and Old Maid. Taking this idea a step further, a deck commissioned in 1951 by the French playing card manufacturer Editions Philibert portrays the Queen of Spades as Lucrezia Borgia (1480-1519). As the Duchess of Ferrara, Lucrezia is identified with the many crimes and sordid activities of the Borgia Family, a powerful dynasty during the Italian Renaissance. These associations give the Queen of Spades a sinister aspect, verging on pure deviance.

To my way of thinking, biblical and historical characters rarely seem appropriate in the context of playing cards, which inhabit a symbolic world of their own. Essentially, it's a world captured by Lewis Carroll in his portrayal of Wonderland. While sometimes the stuff of nightmares, Alice's adventures are always interesting because the fantasy connects in so many unusual ways to the broader realities we all experience every day. The same can be said for the world of playing cards. It, too, models reality. One of the extraordinary things about the deck of cards is that it doesn't tell just one story, it tells many. Playing cards are like a book whose pages are loose, so the story is continually changing as it does in real life. It's a picture book of unbound stories—an intriguing idea.

With all this in mind, rather than a historical character like Lucrezia Borgia or Joan of Arc, it seems the Queen of Spades is better served by the more fanciful character of Morgan le Fay or Morgana. Of course, this is a prominent character in the fifteenth-century retelling of the King Arthur legend, one of the world's truly great faerie tales.

The history of Morgana is tangled in faerie lore and obscured by the revisionist writers of the fourteenth and fifteenth centuries, who did their best to remake her into more of an enchantress and less of a faerie character. Today we think of Morgana as a sorceress and as such, she joins the Spade suit as its Queen, a title acquired in the Arthur stories. A sorceress might seem too fanciful a character for the average person to identify with. People don't think in these terms today, nor do they think in terms of Kings and Queens. In card reading, we use these storybook characters to represent personality types. Essentially, they are symbols, so let's look at a sorceress in that context. This character is typically portrayed in children's stories as a woman who casts magical spells and conjures spirits to do her bidding, all of which seems rather farfetched in modern times. Few of us would consider doing such things, and yet we all try to influence other people every day in one way or another. More often than not, the evil sorceress was trying to do the same thing. From this perspective, Morgana's behavior and its objective are nothing unusual. Basically, she is a manipulator who seeks power over others and tries to control them. As a personality type, I suspect we all have met the Queen of Spades many times.

Morgan Le Fay originated in the Celtic imagination as a water faerie. She is shown as a separate entity, apart from Morgana, in the 5 of Hearts, a compatible suit with Spades. In fact, by flipping their suits signs, a Heart becomes a Spade and vise versa. The concept of reverse images or reflections influenced my approach to both Morgana and Morgan Le Fay, which are really two aspects of the same character.

In folklore, the Morgan was said to haunt lakes and carry away children. Morgan Le Fay comes from this tradition. The 5 of Hearts is associated with Water and the emotions as well as the number 5, which always presents a choice of some kind. We have named this card Fata Morgana, which refers to a type of mirage or illusion created by Water (emotions) and attributed to Morgan Le Fay. In the 5 of Hearts, the real Morgan is seen in her watery reflection, not the alluring illusion she has created for herself.

Putting Morgan Le Fay, a female character, on a male number card, the 5 of Hearts, may seem inappropriate; in this case, however, gender correspondences are irrelevant. The phenomena of Fata Morgana, a mirage over Water, was attributed by early observers to the sorcery of Morgan Le Fay. For our purposes, the connection is of secondary importance. We are primarily interested in the idea of illusions and their manifestation in the Heart suit. The character of Morgan Le Fay is used as a means of illustrating this idea. From that standpoint, there is no conflict in the male/female correspondences. The 5 of Hearts illustrates an idea which, of course, is without gender. The distinction is important.

Another example of this involves the Winds, which are portrayed as male images on female numbers. These cards represent compass points or directions for each suit, along with the corresponding energies associated with these directions. A compass has no gender. On the other hand, the court cards clearly represent people and should be on appropriate male/female numbers. It's really quite simple; people have gender, while concepts like direction or illusion do not.

The Crow Problem

*T*HE SUBJECT OF PLAYING CARDS has been an abiding interest of mine for nearly thirty years. My daughter first showed an interest in the subject when she came for a visit during the summer of 1982. I was living with Ellen Baddler at the time. Everyone called her Lainy, a name she preferred to Ellen. Lainy had studied my ideas on card reading and took Ana with her almost every day to watch her read cards. I barely saw either of them the entire summer.

Anybody who sat down for a reading with Lainy got more than an earful; she talked their ears right off. If you judged a reading by the quantity of information, most everybody got their money's worth. Lainy's fortune-telling muse was a real chatterbox. There were other readings, however, where Lainy said very little and gave her customers more than they could handle.

One time after Lainy finished a reading, the man ran out of his shop and into the street like he had just seen a ghost. When he refused to pay her, a major altercation developed. Lainy finally left when he threatened to call the police. Apparently, she told the man his son was surrounded by a swarm of crows pecking at his head—something to that effect. Lainy often referred to the Spade pip cards as crows. She probably simply assigned a card to the boy and found it in a spread surrounded by Spades. The rest was intuited. Later, we learned the boy, who lived with his mother in Iran, had been diagnosed as having a rare form of brain cancer and was in fact dying. This brings up the question of whether or not the truth is something everyone wants to hear. In this case, the shop owner knew his son was dying but blamed Lainy when she hinted at what he already knew. Generally speaking, good news is something we all want to hear; bad news is another matter. There is a famous story about the Emperor Nero killing every messenger who brought him bad news. I think he killed a half dozen or so before the message got out to the messengers: "Don't give the Emperor bad news." From then on, the news just became better and better; in fact, as Rome burned, the news was positively cheerful. I never told Lainy this story. I probably should have.

Crows were a prominent image in another of Lainy's readings that paid a handsome dividend. One afternoon I received a phone call from a woman who wanted to speak with Lainy. I asked if there was a message, as Lainy wasn't home. The woman said, "Just tell her the lady with the crow problem called."

"The crow problem?"

"Yes, you have that right—the crow problem," came the reply.

"Sounds serious," I said with a laugh.

"Well, yes, it is, or was," the woman responded and added, "When she told me there were crows in my garden eating all my vegetables, I had no idea what that meant. I don't have a garden, but then I got to thinking. I do own a book store..."

I waited for her to continue, trying to visualize crows in her bookstore. I think she read my thoughts. "That's right, crows in my bookstore." The woman went on to explain that after Lainy mentioned the crows eating her vegetables, she started watching her cash register and caught an employee stealing. "Honestly, without Lainy, I wouldn't have had a clue."

Shortly thereafter, Lainy received a fifty-dollar gift certificate from the woman as a show of her appreciation. One gift deserved another.

The Two-Headed Monster

*M*Y DAUGHTER AND I STARTED WORKING TOGETHER on the concepts involved in card reading in 1993. Turned out there was much to be done. Fortunately, the deck of playing cards acted like the foundation of a building and dictated a specific type of construction. We literally built a house of card correspondences on top of this foundation designed centuries ago by some unknown architect.

Both Lainy and Laddy LaDoux (another female friend of mine) read cards, lots of cards in various venues, and used my system over a period of years. They let me know what worked and what didn't. I gained invaluable insights from both these women, but neither of them could help me with the nuts and bolts of building the actual concepts used in reading playing cards. The conceptual work was all mine, until my daughter got involved. Here, at long last, was the person needed to complete my project, which had proceeded by fits and starts for decades and cried out for a fresh point of view.

It is amazing how we can all look at something nearly every day of our lives and never see the thing for what it really is. By looking carefully at playing cards, you can discover clues to the deck's function in divination. Surely everyone can see there are fifty-two cards in a deck, but evidently few people think about the significance of that number. If they did, they might make the connection to a calendar, which divides the year into fifty-two weeks. Why can't we see what is right in front of us? In truth, it is not that easy. To see with understanding is the key.

Working conceptually is mostly a linear process, where one idea begets another and leads you down a road. Unfortunately, all too often, the road leads to a dead end. Other times, ideas pop up miraculously in a non-linear fashion, unimpeded by conscious roadblocks. Dreams speak in a non-linear picture language and sometimes present little puzzles that reveal their meanings in unexpected ways. I've often thought this is the true language of divination and should be used more frequently by those who read cards. If someone doesn't understand right away, that is how it should be. Advise them to think about it awhile. The meaning will reveal itself in time. I'm reminded of Lainy telling the woman about the crows in her garden. The woman didn't comprehend her message until later and gave Lainy all the credit for solving an unforeseen problem.

I remember one time I had a dream, in which this strange character was sitting cross-legged in the middle of a crowded sidewalk with some cards laid out in front of him. People were walking over the cards as they passed by but for some reason, this didn't seem to bother the man much. He just sat there smiling. When I suggested to him that it might be wise to sit somewhere else so that people would not walk over his cards, I was told the cards in front of him were not the problem. It was the cards that he didn't have that created the problem. I wrote the dream down and discussed it at length with my daughter the next day. At first glance, it doesn't seem like much is going on in the dream, but it started her thinking about suit voids, which are found in almost every spread. This became a key concept in our system of card reading. Sometimes the cards that aren't there have just as much importance as the cards that are. The dream brought this to our attention.

It is rare a father and daughter can share a subject so completely that they think as two hemispheres of the same brain, one informing the other. For me, the synergy of our ideas produced revelations. Ana researched geomancy and found additional correspondences that enliven the Four-card spread. She also developed the Sixteen-card spread, which substantially expands the amount of information available in a single reading. Her insights into card meanings as they relate to elements and numbers and her work with suit voids and suit partnerships were equally valuable. All of this was done with sensitivity to the dictates of the deck's calendar and its structure. Ana's many contributions brought the entire system up to critical mass. No doubt, this is now a two-headed monster.

About the Authors

A rare father–daughter team, Ana Cortez and C.J. Freeman combine their talents to bring forth *The Playing Card Oracles.* Sharing a life-long fascination for prophecy and the divinatory arts, both have felt strongly guided in their work together. C.J. Freeman passed away in 2010. Ana resides in Santa Fe, New Mexico where she continues to write and publish her father's artwork for cards.

You may write to Ana c/o Two Sisters Press, P.O. Box 5613, Santa Fe, New Mexico 87502. Her website is www.anacortez.com.